The Lavender Lover's Handbook

The Lavender Lover's Handbook

The 100 Most Beautiful and Fragrant Varieties for
Growing, Crafting, and Cooking

Sarah Berringer Bader

Photographs by Janet Loughrey

Timber Press
Portland • London

Frontispiece: Lavender thriving on a raised berm;
this page: Lavandula angustifolia varieties in a mixed
border; page 6: A field at Lavender at Stonegate.

Published in 2012 by Timber Press, Inc.

The Haseltine Building
133 S.W. Second Avenue, Suite 450
Portland, Oregon 97204-3527
timberpress.com

2 The Quadrant
135 Salusbury Road
London NW6 6RJ
timberpress.co.uk

Printed in China

Library of Congress Cataloging-in-Publication Data

Bader, Sarah Berringer.
    The lavender lover's handbook : the 100 most beautiful
and fragrant varieties for growing, crafting, and cooking /
Sarah Berringer Bader ; photographs by Janet Loughrey. —
1st ed.
        p. cm.
    Includes bibliographical references and index.
    ISBN 978-1-60469-221-1
    1. Lavenders. 2. Cooking (Lavender) 3. Floral
decorations. I. Loughrey, Janet. II. Title.
    SB317.L37B33 2012
    635.9'3396—dc23
                                        2011032472
A catalog record for this book is also available from the
British Library.

To Jerre Ann with love

Contents

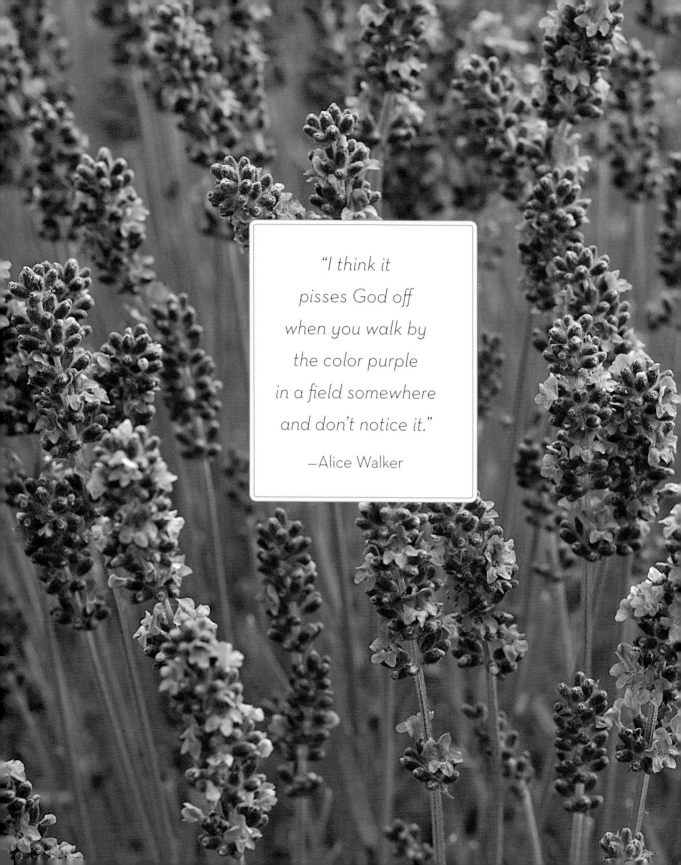

"*I think it
pisses God off
when you walk by
the color purple
in a field somewhere
and don't notice it.*"

—Alice Walker

Preface

Very few plants in the world today tantalize the senses like lavender. I have watched countless people, on a warm summer's day, stop and stare in wonderment at a lavender plant in full bloom. As the fragrance wafts up to your nose, you notice the beautiful color that surrounds the blossoming plant. Next you notice all the bees moving from flower to flower, searching for pollen. If you allow yourself to be still long enough, the faint buzzing of these pollinators will mesmerize you while you take it all in. A full-faculty overload. I think that's what drew me to love lavender in the first place. One day I was out watering a large lavender bush in my yard, and the gentle fragrance filled my nostrils and put me into a trance. I had a sense of calm for the next thirty minutes and couldn't get that experience out of my brain.

At the time, I was working as a recruiter but decided to leave when I had children. I spent more time working on the farm and realized that getting my hands in the dirt filled my soul like nothing else had. I was fortunate enough to acquire a wide spectrum of lavender starts from a local grower and began propagating them. My business, Lavender at Stonegate, began when I was able to successfully grow and sell these beautiful varieties of lavender in both the retail and the wholesale trade.

Once lavender became my full-time job, I would get asked the same questions over and over again by visitors to my farm. People wanted to grow lavender, but they couldn't understand why their plant had become woody, or they couldn't decide which variety would work in their space. If you have questions like these, this book is for you.

I have included detailed facts about lavender cultivars available in North America, as well as information that will help you pick the right plant for your favorite sunny spot. Questions about pruning, spacing, and planting requirements are covered in depth. I have also included some suggestions about how to use lavender in your everyday life. My sincere hope is that this information will allow you to enjoy lavender in a multitude of ways. Being able to grow lavender and use it for the abundant purposes for which it is suited is a joy I hope more and more people can embrace.

Acknowledgments

To the Creator, who gave me the task of adding just a little more beauty to the world.

My kiddos, Jake and Hannah, who make everything worth it.

To my family for all your love and support.

To Janet Loughrey, my photographer, who did an amazing job with the photos.

To Juree Sondker, my editor, for keeping me on task and for your gentle guidance.

To Susyn Andrews and Tim Upson for *The Genus Lavandula*, a publication we refer to as the lavender bible.

To Art Tucker and the late Thomas DeBaggio for *The Encyclopedia of Herbs* (the most recent edition of *The Big Book of Herbs*). This and *The Genus Lavandula* have been invaluable in my quest for information.

To the proprietors of several breathtaking farms in Sequim, Washington, including Purple Haze Lavender Farm, The Cutting Garden, Le Jardin de Soleil, and Sunshine Herb and Lavender Farm, who allowed us to take photos.

To Andy and Melissa Van Hevelingen, with sincere admiration and appreciation, for your knowledge of and commitment to lavender varieties and for producing so many beautiful cultivars for the rest of us to enjoy.

To Don Roberts for your guidance and for three of my favorite lavenders.

Many thanks to Chris Mulder of Barn Owl Nursery for your knowledge about so many things lavender, for allowing us to take pictures at your place, and for the much-needed advice on cooking with lavender.

To Barbara Remington for your words of encouragement and for your long history with this wonderful herb.

To Joy Creek Nursery for allowing us to take pictures of your beautiful grounds.

A big thank you to Dot Carson, Stacey Hanf, and Jane Mannex for allowing us to take photos of your stunning gardens and to Kim Pokorny of *The Oregonian* for putting the word out to find them.

To Doug Schmidt of Purple Dog Lavender Farm for your delicious crème brûlée recipe.

To Eleanor Suman from Eleanor's Signature Catering for sharing your recipe for lavender chocolate truffles.

Many thanks to Janice and Carol of Morrow's Flowers for making our beautiful lavender creations.

To Michael for always believing in me.

And last but not least, to my tribe, who show me how to live life with grace and integrity.

Page 8: *Lavandula angustifolia* 'Betty's Blue'; opposite: Jardin du Soleil, Sequim, Washington

Lavender Obsession:

An Introduction

Lavender fields, Purple
Haze Lavender Farm,
Sequim, Washington

On a warm, sunny day, it doesn't get much better than brushing up against a lavender plant and inhaling the intoxicating aroma. You can experience this just about anywhere in your landscape. From pathways to rock gardens, lavender makes a wonderful focal point, and it is useful as well. Any warm, sunny spot will do, as long as the soil allows for proper drainage and the plant gets plenty of room to grow.

There are more than 450 named lavender varieties or cultivars, and more are being discovered all the time. Lavender belongs to the Lamiaceae, the mint family, which includes oregano, sage, and other fragrant herbs. There are several species within the genus *Lavandula*, grouping plants together based on characteristics such as hardiness, leaf shape, and fragrance. Some species are available only in certain parts of the world, and only about four species can be grown outside of tropical climates.

What Makes Lavender a Great Addition to the Landscape?

Lavender is a beautiful addition to just about any garden. Lavender foliage colors range from various shades of green through gray-green to silver; variegated cultivars are even available. The flowers are not just lavender but come in a spectrum of color from blues and purples to whites and pinks. These plants also come in a variety of sizes: there are dwarf lavenders, medium-sized lavenders, and lavenders that grow quite large to fit into any landscape design. More and more people are realizing how easy lavender is to grow and how useful it can be in the garden.

Once lavender is established, it doesn't need to be watered very often. Plants are considered drought tolerant if they can survive a dry period with little or no supplemental watering. With lavender's sunny disposition, it certainly falls into this category. In fact, when lavender is placed in the right spot—where it has full sun, good drainage, and plenty of room to grow—it will thrive with very little care, even through the summer months. With many municipalities restricting water use, these plants can hold their own and help conserve water.

Lavender attracts a wide range of pollinators that are not only benefi-

Lavender planted with drought-tolerant poppies and euphorbia

Lavandula angustifolia 'Sachet' with bee balm and sedums, Stacey Hanf garden, St. Helens, Oregon

Herb garden with
lavender, Dot Carson
garden, Tualatin, Oregon

Lavandula stoechas
'Portuguese Giant'
mingled with *L. angustifolia*
'Coconut Ice'

cial to your garden but also great for the environment. A lavender plant draws the bugs you want in your garden that, in turn, eat the ones you don't. On a hot, sunny day, anyone can become mesmerized by watching the level of activity on one lavender plant. Bumblebees, honeybees, butterflies, ladybugs, and praying mantises are only some of the beneficial insects a lavender plant will attract. These pollinator and parasitic species not only help the plants and flowers thrive, they also greatly reduce the need for pesticides throughout your garden.

If you have had deer wander in your yard, you know that they like to nibble on just about anything. The only way to really keep a deer out of your garden permanently is a tall fence, but lavender is considered a deer-resistant plant, meaning they do not prefer the taste of lavender. If hungry enough, they may nibble the tops of young plants a bit, but they normally stay clear of established plants. Rabbits don't like lavender, either.

Lavender plants are built-in aromatherapy. Not only do they add a wonderful fragrance to your garden, but the lavender flowers can also be brought indoors for herbal teas, homemade crafts, and sachets for your drawers. It's hard to think of another plant that can add this much beauty and joy to our lives.

Which Lavender to Plant?

Lavenders come in a wide range of sizes, habits, and bloom colors. The best lavender for you to plant will depend upon both the growing conditions you can offer and the effect you want to achieve in your garden. For a full list of lavenders and their particular characteristics and requirements, see "The Lavender Palette."

Lavender has been grown for centuries in many parts of the world. In North America, however, the lavender industry is still in its infancy. The topography of the United States and Canada is expansive and diverse. To date, very little research has been done to determine which cultivars of lavender can grow well in particular locations. Much of the information gathered on the topic is done by lavender growers who share information among themselves. My hope with this book is to educate gardeners about which types of lavender can grow in these varied climates and how this can be done successfully. Growing lavender can be "iffy" in certain regions of North America where temperatures regularly plunge well below freezing in the winter. And areas with higher humidity during summer months may be limited to growing lavender species that can take these conditions.

If you live in an area that has four seasons, you will have the most success with hardy lavenders. The two hardy lavender species illustrated in

Favorite Lavenders by Bloom Color

If you want lavenders with deep purple, dark blue, or pink blossoms, these cultivars are great choices.

Richest purples

Lavandula angustifolia 'Hidcote'
L. angustifolia 'Hidcote Superior'
L. angustifolia 'Imperial Gem'
L. angustifolia 'Purple Bouquet'
L. ×intermedia 'Impress Purple'

Darkest blues

L. angustifolia 'Betty's Blue'
L. angustifolia 'Blue Cushion'
L. angustifolia 'Thumbelina Leigh'
L. angustifolia 'Violet Intrigue'

Favorite pinks

L. angustifolia 'Coconut Ice'
L. angustifolia 'Hidcote Pink'
L. angustifolia 'Little Lottie'
L. angustifolia 'Melissa'
L. angustifolia 'Miss Katherine'

Best Lavenders for Humid Summers

These lavenders can withstand hotter, more humid temperatures in the summertime.

Lavandula ×chaytorae 'Ana Luisa'
L. ×chaytorae 'Kathleen Elizabeth'
L. ×intermedia 'Grosso'
L. ×intermedia 'Provence'
L. stoechas 'Otto Quast'

Best Cold-Weather Lavenders

These varieties have been proven to withstand colder temperatures and come back year after year.

Lavandula angustifolia 'Buena Vista'
L. angustifolia 'Folgate'
L. angustifolia 'Imperial Gem'
L. angustifolia 'Maillette'
L. angustifolia 'Royal Velvet'

Lavenders with the Strongest Scent

These lavenders are known for their high oil content and strong fragrance. There are fragrant *Lavandula angustifolia* varieties, but they generally have a more delicate, floral note.

Lavandula ×intermedia 'Fat Spike'
L. ×intermedia 'Grosso'
L. ×intermedia 'Hidcote Giant'
L. ×intermedia 'Impress Purple'
L. ×intermedia 'Provence'
L. ×intermedia 'Super'

this book are *Lavandula angustifolia* and *Lavandula ×intermedia*. Most true lavenders or *Lavandula angustifolia* varieties have the same hardiness rating, so if you have success growing *L. angustifolia* 'Betty's Blue', chances are you will have the same success growing *L. angustifolia* 'Royal Velvet'. *Lavandula stoechas* can withstand colder temperatures for short periods of time but are not considered hardy. A few other tender lavender species for warmer climates are included in "The Lavender Palette."

The Range of Lavender Fragrance

Plant fragrance among lavenders is as varied as wine. Each has its own photochemistry, producing a unique combination of naturally occurring chemicals. In general, *Lavandula angustifolia* varieties tend to have a more distinctive floral note. As a result, oil from this species is found in higher-end cosmetics and perfumes. *Lavandula ×intermedia* varieties contain more camphor—a sharper, woodier fragrance—and their oil is used in detergents at a higher volume. *Lavandula stoechas* has a high ketone content, making it particularly pungent. Other factors that affect fragrance include soil, age of the plant, when the lavender is harvested, and even rainfall levels. Which type of lavender fragrance smells best is a matter of personal opinion. Rub the leaves and flowers of different species and varieties in your fingers and discover your own favorites.

Lavender paired with echinacea

Is It English or Is It French?

For the sake of simplicity, it is easy to get into the habit of nicknaming plant species to avoid long, hard-to-pronounce botanical names. Lavender has fallen victim to this process, and terms such as English, French, Spanish, and even German are commonly used to identify particular groups of

Lavandula angustifolia varieties in a mixed border, Joy Creek Nursery, Scappoose, Oregon

lavender. In the United States, we hear *Lavandula stoechas* referred to as Spanish lavender, while in the United Kingdom *L. stoechas* is commonly called French lavender. Here in the states, the common name French lavender is generally used for the species that you would imagine would grow in France, namely *L. ×intermedia*, but French lavender is actually the common name for *L. dentata*, a toothed lavender that is altogether different from *L. ×intermedia*. In Australia, English lavender can mean both *L. angustifolia* and *L. ×intermedia*, and *L. stoechas* is called Italian lavender. In France, *L. angustifolia* is called *la lavande*, yet in other countries it is called English. *Lavandula ×intermedia* 'Dutch' was misread as 'Deutch' along the way and is sometimes referred to as German lavender. Confusing, isn't it?

If you really want to shorten the names for classification, English lavenders or varieties of *Lavandula angustifolia* can be called true or common lavender. Varieties of *L. ×intermedia* are referred to as lavandins. *L. stoechas* is technically French lavender, as it came from the southern coast of France, but using this name can be confusing to someone who has a different idea of what French lavender is. It is probably best to refer to it as stoechas.

Lavender Past and Future

Lavender has been a staple in gardens around the globe for centuries. The earliest accounts on record indicate that lavender was used for a multitude of purposes. In medieval times, powdered lavender was used as a condiment and preservative to mask disagreeable flavors. Plants were introduced in England

Lavandula stoechas with tulips and sedums in a spring border designed by Darcy Daniels

around AD 1265, and cuttings were often used as floor bedding to keep pests away. France has used lavender as a cash crop for the lavender oil industry and produces well in excess of 1,000 tons of lavender essence each year to perfume detergents and the like.

Commercial lavender production began in North America sometime around 1924 in Seattle, Washington. Since then, interest in lavender production has taken root, and some lavender farms have established themselves as tourist destinations. As more farmers are realizing the value of growing this wondrous herb, lavender farms in several regions across the United States have joined forces to offer collective tours for visitors to enjoy.

With more and more people incorporating alternative methods of healing and wellness, lavender is making a stand thanks to its wide range of uses in cooking, crafting, aromatherapy, and the like. I have included a few things to try in this book, but you will find many more suggestions in other books, in magazines, and on the web.

Lavender in the Garden:

Landscapes, Containers, and Herb Gardens

Lavandula angustifolia varieties in a mixed border at Joy Creek Nursery, Scappoose, Oregon

As you contemplate how to use lavender in your garden, one place to start is to think about where it might be happiest. Certain areas of your landscape may be more conducive to growing lavender than others simply because they provide more heat, drainage, or wind protection. You can use these microclimates to your advantage when planting lavender.

Think as well about planting lavender with other ornamentals that withstand drought and that complement lavender in color, height, and bloom habit. You can do this in borders and hedges as well as in rock gardens, knot gardens, and containers. Lavender is also a natural planted with other herbs in a container or bed near your kitchen door for easy snipping.

Microclimates for Growing Lavender

Microclimates are places where climatic conditions vary from the region as a whole. These can be as small as a garden bed in your backyard or as large as a 600-square-mile peninsula. A microclimate may get more sunshine or less rainfall than the general area in which it's located, allowing gardeners to succeed with plants that are technically out of their natural range. For example, your climate zone may be considered too cold to grow lavender, but a row of lavender planted along a concrete pathway may nonetheless thrive thanks to the heat the concrete releases.

Microclimates are affected by topography, bodies of water, and urban areas. Backyard microclimates are created by buildings and structures, paved surfaces, raised beds and containers, and sunny nooks. You can take advantage of your knowledge about local microclimates to help you grow lavender successfully.

Topography outlines the general features of a particular region. This could be an entire mountainside or a section of your backyard. Walk around your yard in the winter and check out which sections are sunnier and which ones dip into a colder area. If there are slopes, does one side get lots of sunlight and the other side less? A south-facing hill that draws more sunlight during the day can give lavender the heat it needs even if the rest of your yard is more shaded and cooler. Lavender needs full sun for at least six hours a day in order to thrive. So if you plant your lavender on a south-facing wall outside your home or a southern slope on a hillside in your backyard it will have a better chance of flourishing.

Are there trees along a hillside that could block sunlight? Hills can also block wind and redirect air currents, holding in both moisture and pockets of cool air. If you want to provide wind protection for your plants, planting on a hill can be beneficial, but make sure the hill does not block sunlight. Keep in mind that heat rises, while cold air falls. A valley or the bottom of a slope in your yard will expose plants to colder temperatures.

Areas along large bodies of water, such as the Great Lakes or the Atlantic Ocean, have temperatures averaging 5 to 10 degrees warmer than those areas away from water. These regions by water are less prone to late springs and early frosts because the body of water moderates the surrounding air temperature. The added moisture in the air creates a mini-greenhouse effect by trapping the infrared radiation reflected from the earth. Smaller water sources like ponds can have the same effect in your backyard. If you have a water source nearby, your average temperatures may be higher than in the rest of your zone.

Urban landscapes create extra heat generated from the vast amount of concrete and stone in the environment. The buildings and paved surfaces absorb solar radiation during the day and release it at night. This means that if you live in the city, your growing temperatures will be a full zone higher than those in surrounding rural areas. Container gardening on an

Lavender and poppies, Jardin du Soleil, Sequim, Washington

Lavandula ×*intermedia*
'Grosso' and 'Provence'
in Stacey Hauf's garden,
St. Helens, Oregon

apartment balcony can offer plants warmer temperatures due to the fact that heat rises.

In your backyard, planting lavender next to a building, such as a house or barn, will add charm to the landscape. Buildings will provide wind protection during colder months. Bringing plants closer to a structure will keep them warmer, thus allowing you to grow plants through the winter that may not have survived otherwise. But buildings can also throw shade on planting areas, so make sure the spot you choose gets at least six hours of sunlight a day. Too much shade will stunt lavender plants and inhibit flowering. Keep your rain gutters clean and free of debris so as to avoid spilling rainwater onto plants growing below.

Structures such as rock walls or gazebos will also provide protection from the elements and create a pretty backdrop for lavender. Rock walls go hand in hand with lavender, especially if you want to create a Mediterranean look. A formal gazebo with lavender and roses makes a stunning focal point, and the combination of fragrances on a warm summer day is intoxicating. Just make sure your plants receive adequate sunshine, drainage, and room to grow.

Raised beds for lavender allow you to use microclimates to your advantage, first because you can choose soil that will benefit the plant and second because these containers can be placed in the most ideal locations for aesthetics and adequate sunshine. Placing a container next to a wall or on a patio will create wind and frost protection while keeping the plants close by for easy inspection.

There may be sunny spots in your garden that are sheltered by large rocks or other natural barriers. These spots may give you the opportunity to grow plants for many years that would otherwise not be suited to your yard. Experiment with creating an environment of full sun, good

Lavandula ×intermedia 'Fred Boutin' in a mixed border at Village Green, Cottage Grove, Oregon

Raised herb bed in Dot Carson's garden, Tualatin, Oregon, designed by Phil Thornburg of Winterbloom

drainage, and frost protection. Unusually harsh winters can eventually kill plants even in sunny nooks, but it certainly doesn't hurt to try.

Planting Lavender with Other Drought-Tolerant Plants

Lavender is a natural in a landscape with other drought-tolerant plants. These plants tend to come from dry regions such as the Mediterranean and central Asia. They require well-drained soil and can even thrive in poor soils, provided they have plenty of sun throughout the day. The fact that they all have similar watering requirements makes it easier to remember how often to water them.

Planting lavender with other similar sun-loving plants can have additional benefits as well. Companion planting is the idea of grouping two or more kinds of plants together to enjoy the benefits these similar types of plants can offer. Many drought-tolerant plants attract the "good bugs" you want in your landscape. Herbs are also great compadres to lavender and are discussed later in this chapter.

Drought-tolerant plants come in a wide spectrum of colors, shapes, heights, and bloom times. The following list includes drought-tolerant ornamental plants that complement lavender in color, height, and bloom habit.

Achillea millefolium (yarrow) is native to the Northern Hemisphere and blooms in many colors including white, yellow, pink, and even red. Yarrow is beneficial to the soil and attracts insects such as ladybugs and hoverflies. Some popular cultivars to try include 'Cerise Queen' and 'Red Beauty', and the hybrid 'Paprika'.

Arabis species (rockcress) are low-growing perennials that are a great pick for rock gardens, borders, or as a ground cover. In spring, they burst with lots of fragrant blooms in whites, pinks, and lavenders.

Armeria maritima (thrift, sea pink) forms a grasslike tuft with stems 2 to 3 inches high. There are approximately 20 varieties on the market ranging from white to pink to cherry-red. Considered ultrahardy from zone 2.

Artemisia species (wormwood, sagebrush) are a good choice to add silver foliage to your landscape. They bloom bright yellow in midsummer. Soft to the touch, *Artemisia* needs to be trimmed back or it can get a bit out of control. *Artemisia schmidtiana* 'Silver Mound' is a foot-high variety with finely cut, silvery white leaves.

Centranthus ruber (Jupiter's beard, red valerian) offers fragrant, dome-shaped flowers in white or dark pink and can reach 2 to 3 feet high. This is a fast grower that self-sows and can be considered invasive if not trimmed back properly.

Cerastium tomentosum (snow in summer) has silver foliage and lots of white flowers in early summer. This plant is commonly grown in zones 3–7 but can be grown in zones 8–10. It is important to trim flowers back after blooming as they will quickly reseed.

Echeveria species (hen and chicks) are succulents that are extremely easy to grow and prolific multipliers. The "hen plant" produces baby chicks that can be removed and placed elsewhere in the garden to make more plants. They come in reds, pinks, and bright greens and flower in summer.

Echinacea purpurea (purple coneflower) has large purple-pink daisylike flowers with 2- to 5-foot stems that can grow just about anywhere. Coneflowers have grown in popularity with their use in herbal teas. Echinacea sows seeds freely.

Lavender with drought-tolerant gaillardia and sedum

Gallardia grandiflora (blanket flower) has flower heads that are bright burnt orange tipped with yellow. These summer bloomers grow up to 2 feet tall.

Kniphofia uvaria (red-hot poker) has flame-colored spikes that reach 2 to 5 feet high and flower colors ranging from ivory and orange to coral red. Put them in the background for height and to draw the eye to the back of your garden.

Lithodora diffusa grows as a dark green mat of foliage with deep blue, almost iridescent flowers starting in early summer. This is a great lavender complement, especially planted around in rock gardens, borders, and large containers. It blossoms throughout the summer, and in mild climates will even bloom in the winter.

Oenothera species (evening primrose) are native to North America and can be used as an easy-care spreading ground cover. The yellow or pink flowers open in the evenings and close at dawn. These plants are useful for filling a barren area in a rock garden with bright color.

Chicken coop planted with *Lavandula ×intermedia* 'Provence' and 'Nathalie Nypels' rose

Penstemon species (beard tongue) include a few hundred varieties. Hummingbirds love them because of their attractive trumpet-shaped blooms. These come in whites, pinks, and even purples, making it easy to create interesting color schemes with them. Penstemons come in a multitude of sizes and habits as well.

Rudbeckia hirta (black-eyed Susan) is a biennial with flowers that reach up to 3 feet tall and resemble mini-sunflowers in color and height. Black-eyed Susans grow in clusters and are quite an eye-catcher when grown en masse. Use them as an anchor plant in rock gardens or perennial beds.

Sedum species (stonecrop) are succulents with flowers in yellow, orange, red, or pink that appear in late summer to early fall. The leaves stay stunning throughout the year, and they make a great focal plant. 'Autumn Joy' is a favorite cultivar with pink flowers that fade to rusty brown. *Sedum spurium* (two-row stonecrop) has bright green foliage with red margins; the cultivar 'Dragon's Blood' has showy pink to deep red flowers in summer.

Lavender and roses can make great companion plants. Roses tend to attract aphids, while ladybugs love lavender. When lavender attracts these aphid-eating insects, you have instant organic pest control. Roses like well-drained soil, just like lavender. Some antique roses can tolerate heat extremes better than others. For hotter climates, try planting *Lavandula ×intermedia* varieties with teas, Chinas, and hybrid musks. Roses such as Kordes breeder series and rugosas are bred for colder climates and would do well with hardier *L. angustifolia* and *L. ×intermedia* varieties.

Make sure you check the planting, spacing, and watering requirements of the rose you choose before planting with lavender. According to *Rose Magazine*, no modern hybrid roses can be considered drought tolerant. Certain tender varieties of roses may need to be watered more than others. That said, you can practice some techniques during hotter months that will reduce the need to water. Mulching roses with 3 to 4 inches of compost will provide increased water retention, allowing you to water less when warm weather hits.

Borders and Hedges

Lavender is a good choice for creating curb appeal. A lavender hedge along a driveway or sidewalk can add color and fragrance that will entice the senses and set the tone for the rest of the yard. Planting a row of lavenders up a driveway creates a welcome cottage feel. Do you want your lavender-

Lavandula angustifolia varieties mixed with spirea and smokebush along a gravel path, Joy Creek Nursery

planted driveway or sidewalk to show color throughout the summer? Then plant continuous-blooming varieties such as *Lavandula angustifolia* 'Sharon Roberts' or 'French Fields'. Larger *L. ×intermedia* cultivars such as 'Fred Boutin' or 'Fragrant Memories' create uniform hedges that bloom later in the summer. For an earlier bloomer with a vibrant lilac bloom, try *L. angustifolia* 'Royal Purple'.

You can use any lavender for hedging; however, larger lavenders that grow 3 feet tall or higher are ideal for a true hedging effect. Giving these larger lavenders plenty of space to grow and bloom is essential, not only to prevent overcrowding but also to give you enough room to move up and down the driveway with ease. Make sure that when you space your lavender plants, you make allowances for when the plants bloom. *Lavandula ×intermedia* 'Grosso' will be about 3 feet high most of the year, but during bloom season the stems grow as long as 18 inches on all sides, so keep this in mind when measuring your planting area.

Just keep in mind that lavender in bloom can tempt a passerby to clip a few sprigs without your permission. If you want to keep your lavender intact throughout the summer, you might want to plant it in an area that is not as accessible. If your border is along a building, keep in mind things like spacing, light, drainage, and foundation issues that may affect not only your plants but your home as well.

Lavenders planted in a border with other sun-loving plants can spice up your yard while attracting bees for pollination. When designing a border with lavender and other plants, remember to read the mature size and growth rate of the plants you are considering. A 2-foot tree could eventually become a 40-foot tree, creating foundation problems if next to a building and throwing shade on sun-loving plants. For an even layout, plant taller specimens in the back, while giving medium-sized plants enough space to fill in the desired spot. If you want some variation and color while your perennials mature, consider interspersing annuals to fill in naked spaces.

Picking the right lavender for your space is important because some get rather large and can crowd other plants in your landscape. It is tempting to want instant beautification and to plant your lavender too close together to fill in your space, but in a few years your plants will crowd together and hamper air circulation. This could cause mildew and root rot, which could shorten the life of your plants. It is better to buy larger plants to begin with, or space them accordingly and be patient. Make sure your plant has adequate room on all sides for even growth and full flowering. Lavender usually doubles in size every year until year three and will continue to grow beyond that depending on the variety.

A row of *Lavandula ×intermedia* 'Grosso' lining a driveway at Barn Owl Nursery, Wilsonville, Oregon

Lavandula angustifolia
'Graves' backed by taller
Phygelius 'Yellow Trumpet'
in a mixed border at Joy
Creek Nursery

More lavenders in a
mixed border at
Joy Creek Nursery

Earliest Bloomers

The first to flower in the season, these lavenders will add color to your garden when springtime arrives.

Lavandula angustifolia 'Bowles Early'
L. angustifolia 'Croxton's Wild'
L. angustifolia 'Folgate'
L. angustifolia 'French Fields'
L. angustifolia 'Tucker's Early'

Best Lavenders for Hedges

To create a hedge using lavender, try these larger lavenders.

Lavandula angustifolia 'Royal Purple'
L. ×intermedia 'Alba'
L. ×intermedia 'Fragrant Memories'
L. ×intermedia 'Fred Boutin'
L. ×intermedia 'Grappenhall'
L. ×intermedia 'Grosso'
L. ×intermedia 'Provence'

All-Season Bloomers

For lavender that blooms more than once in a season, try these hardworking cultivars.

Lavandula angustifolia 'Buena Vista'
L. angustifolia 'Croxton's Wild'
L. angustifolia 'French Fields'
L. angustifolia 'Sharon Roberts'
L. stoechas 'Madrid Purple'
L. stoechas 'Spanish Curly Top'

Best Lavenders for Containers

Smaller and more compact, these cultivars are great for planting in your favorite containers.

Lavandula angustifolia 'Blue River'
L. angustifolia 'Dwarf Blue'
L. angustifolia 'Hidcote Superior'
L. angustifolia 'Lavenite Petite'
L. angustifolia 'Little Lottie'
L. angustifolia 'Thumbelina Leigh'

Rock garden with *Lavandula angustifolia* flanked by erigeron and eryngium on the left and ornamental golden oregano on the right, Stacey Hanf garden

Rock Gardens

A rock garden is essentially a featured area, usually sloped, with irregular rock formations that contain a collection of plants and herbs. Most perennial plants bloom in the spring, so adding additional herbs and shrubs that provide color throughout the summer will enhance your space. Most plants in a rock garden have a few things in common. First, they need full sun and good drainage. Second, they have a general theme or uniformity to them that provides texture and color.

When you build a rock garden, the type of rocks you choose will determine the plants that go with it. For instance, if you want a garden with red sandstone, put in specimens that have foliage or flowers with hints of red and colors that complement red. Native rock types will be more readily available. You can purchase a range of sizes from landscape contractors and rock dealers. Rock gardens usually create elevation above an existing site. This involves laying a foundation of larger rocks and then interspersing smaller rocks in the design to achieve height and depth.

It is tempting to rush to your local garden center and buy a hodgepodge of plants to fill in the space, but this can make the rock garden look too busy and take away from the rock formations you are trying to accent. Rock garden plants are meant to complement the infrastructure, not dominate the planting space. Smaller lavenders can be used as anchor plants in the center, while larger lavenders can add height around the edges.

Remember to stick with color schemes that go well together. I like to use trailing ground cover in complementary colors and low-growing perennials to match. *Lavandula angustifolia* 'Betty's Blue' makes a wonderful accent plant with *Lithodora diffusa* 'Grace Ward'. Lithodora flowers brilliant blue in early spring, and 'Betty's Blue' flowers shortly thereafter. Silver plants such as *Stachys byzantina* (lamb's ear) grow well with *Campanula carpatica* f. *alba* 'Weisse Clips' for color and foliage variation. Adding splashes of blues, yellows, or purples throughout will create an eye-catching garden spot.

Lavandula angustifolia 'Mitchum Gray' accented with *Penstemon* 'Firebird' and *Hypericum olympicum*, Joy Creek Nursery

Some plants may grow too big for the space and may need to be divided or replanted. Weeds can be an issue in rock gardens; mulching is the answer, but wood chips may look out of place so a great alternative is to mulch with gravel or pebbles in the same color as your foundation rocks. Remember to use well-draining soil and add compost at planting.

Knot Gardens

A knot garden is a formal garden planted with dwarf hedges of evergreens laid out in intricate geometric patterns. The knots created in these elaborate garden designs in Tudor England, where knot gardens originated, represented the tying together of elements. Knots were also symbols of marriage as the tying together of two families. In earlier garden designs, plants were woven in carefully planned works of art to resemble the threads of ancient Celtic knot work.

Traditional knot gardens require a great deal of maintenance and were replaced in modern times by a variation known as parterre. This less labor-intensive layout still incorporates a knot design, yet the foliage does not twist together as with earlier styles. Most knot gardens use a base of hardy boxwood such as *Buxus microphylla* 'Winter Gem' and incorporate various perennials throughout the design. Most are planted so they may be easily viewed from a window or as a focal point in a courtyard. Designs can be as simple or as elaborate as you choose. Modern-day knot gardens feature colorful corresponding plants in a mass of colors and sizes. They can be as small or as large as you can imagine for your space.

Preparation is key to a successful layout. Choose an area with full sun in a location that you will be able to view often, preferably from above, such as a level spot close to the house. If you use sun-loving plants that bloom at different times throughout the year, your knot garden will always have color. Lavender is a great choice for knot gardens for many reasons. You can choose plants that bloom when you want them to, to complement other plants. Even in winter months, lavender forms uniform evergreen mounds that create order throughout your space.

Labyrinths, a form of knot garden, have increased in popularity in

Labyrinth garden with lavender, designed by Laura Crockett

recent years. The ancient labyrinth goes back several thousand years, and examples of these mazes are featured in cathedrals and archaic gardens around the globe. A labyrinth consists of a single nonbranching path that leads in a spiral pattern to the center and is easy to navigate. Many people have incorporated labyrinths in their gardens to practice meditation, as walking a labyrinth allows one to tune out the outside world and achieve a meditative state. Lavender, with its calming aroma, is a fitting plant to include in a labyrinth garden.

Container Gardens

Raised beds or containers are a great way to create the right environment to grow lavender. If your soil is hard to work with, making your own habitation for plants lets you put in just the right soil to create proper drainage. You can strategically place these beds where they get the optimal amount of sunshine (at least six hours a day), giving you a better chance of growing a happy lavender plant. Placing a container up against a house or a structure will give it adequate wind protection during colder months.

Growing in containers also reduces the soil compaction that can happen when your beds are at ground level. Weeding a container garden can be much easier than tackling a larger planting space, especially since the

Lavandula angustifolia planted with dwarf petunias in a half wine barrel

Lavender planted with
thyme and golden
oregano

plants are raised and easier to get to. And if your gardening space is limited, containers can allow you to grow lavender even on a rooftop or patio.

Make sure your raised bed is large enough to hold a plant that is full
grown. Most lavenders can grow up to 3 feet around or more, so keep this
in mind when planning your planting space. If you start out with a lavender in a 4-inch pot, the plant will double every year until year three, when
it will grow two-thirds bigger than year two. Keeping your younger plant
in a smaller container in the first year with other plants is okay, but make
sure you transplant it the following year to a bigger pot or into the ground.

Lavender looks fantastic in half wine barrels. The diameter of these
barrels is the perfect size for lavender and they make a statement all by
themselves. You can always plant other low-growing plants around them
such as sedums or pansies. Adding a spring bloomer to your lavender container will ensure you will have something blooming all summer long.

Lavender likes a long, good soak every few weeks when planted in containers. Most people water more frequently but don't water long enough to
get down to the roots. You may need to give it a little water and then walk
away to give it a few minutes to soak in, then water again.

Lavender, rosemary, sage, and other herbal edibles

Edible Herb Gardens

More and more people are realizing the benefit of growing their own herbs for culinary use. Herbs can be dried and saved for later or used fresh right out of the garden. Lavender requires the same care as many other herbs. It likes well-draining soil, full sun, and occasional pruning throughout the summer. Are there particular recipes you use that call for fresh herbs? If so, those may be the herbs you want to include in your planting. Keep a large container of planted herbs you use frequently near your kitchen door so you can easily snip a few sprigs when cooking.

One can never have enough basil. Rosemary, oregano, and thyme are staples, but trying new ones like lemon verbena for teas will broaden your palate. Be careful when planting mint varieties as they will spread and take over your planting space. To avoid that, plant mints in the ground in a pot to keep them contained. Most perennial herbs will grow large, so read the spacing requirements when planting.

The Lavender Palette:

100 Varieties to Try

The rich palette of *Lavandula* ×*intermedia* 'Grosso' and other cultivars

Whrat follows is an annotated and illustrated list of 100 lavender varieties that vary in size, color, and fragrance for you to choose from. Each cultivar has its own appeal. I encourage you to try as many as you can get your hands on. For each variety, you'll find the origin, the flower and bloom colors, the stem length, information about bloom frequency and timing and about plant height and spacing, and the hardiness rating. Some varieties of lavender are protected by a plant patent, which means that their propagation for commercial use by anyone other than licensed growers is prohibited.

Origin

Some lavenders are specifically bred for a particular characteristic, while others are discovered by chance and eventually named. A good number of the lavender cultivars listed here were carefully selected and brought to North America; others were chance seedlings that caught the eye of plant breeders and were named accordingly. Knowing the origin of a plant is part of appreciating its unique qualities.

Flower and Foliage Color

To help you find the right hue of lavender for your garden space or container, each entry in the lavender palette gives a flower color and a foliage color. You can best visualize these colors by referring to the color guides included here, which will give you an approximate idea of what each color term means. If you want more precision in matching plant colors, you may want to consult the RHS (Royal Horticultural Society) Colour Chart, a standardized reference guide to hundreds of colors in nature, in conjunction with *The Genus Lavandula* by Tim Upson and Susyn Andrews, which labels hundreds of individual cultivars by exact color based on the 1986 RHS chart. You can purchase color charts from the Royal Horticultural Society website (www.rhs.org.uk/Plants/RHS-Publications/RHS-colour-charts) in a full version or a mini version.

Sarah's Top Picks

If I had to choose the ten best lavender varieties, these are the ones I'd put on that list.

✳ *Lavandula angustifolia* 'Betty's Blue'
The first wreath I ever made was with 'Betty's Blue', and the plant is still a top choice for wreaths I make today. The flower heads hold together well for drying, and the deep blue color is captivating.

✳ *Lavandula angustifolia* 'Buena Vista'
A super sweet fragrance and rich purple flowers on a plant that blooms all summer—what more could you ask for? 'Buena Vista' is also a great choice for culinary use.

✳ *Lavandula angustifolia* 'Folgate'
This is my all-around favorite lavender. 'Folgate' can withstand colder temperatures and is one of the first to bloom in the season. The soft periwinkle blue flowers are my first choice for fresh cut, and the plant has a tight bloom habit that looks great all year long.

✳ *Lavandula angustifolia* 'Melissa'
Pink lavenders are known for their sweet fragrance, and 'Melissa' is no exception. This cultivar is a top pick for use in your favorite recipes.

✳ *Lavandula angustifolia* 'Purple Bouquet'
If you want a deep, rich purple flower combined with long stems, this lavender is an excellent choice. 'Purple Bouquet' also blooms twice during the season.

✳ *Lavandula angustifolia* 'Royal Purple'
This larger-than-life lavender makes a statement. Boasting hundreds of long-stemmed light purple flowers, it makes an excellent choice for a hedge or a focal point in the garden.

✳ *Lavandula angustifolia* 'Royal Velvet'
As its name suggests, this lavender has a rich, velvety flower head, along with long stems for crafts. One of the top picks for all-around great lavender.

✳ *Lavandula ×chaytorae* 'Ana Luisa'
All who see 'Ana Luisa' blooming have to have one for their collection. The combination of light silvery foliage and long, deep purple blossoms is stunning. 'Ana Luisa' can withstand higher humidity in the summer, making it a good choice for warm, humid climates.

✳ *Lavandula ×intermedia* 'Gros Bleu'
'Gros Bleu' combines the rich color of the *angustifolias* with the bloom habit and long stems of lavandin varieties. Because it has less camphor than other lavandins, it has a light, clean lavender scent.

✳ *Lavandula ×intermedia* 'Grosso'
When customers ask which lavender has the strongest scent, this is the lavender I recommend. 'Grosso' is also the preferred cultivar for wands and sachets.

Flower Color Guide

WHITE
Lavandula ×intermedia
'Edelweiss'

LIGHT PINK
Lavandula angustifolia
'Hidcote Pink'

PINK
Lavandula angustifolia
'Miss Katherine'

DARK BLUE
Lavandula angustifolia
'Betty's Blue'

LIGHT PURPLE
Lavandula ×intermedia
'Silver Leaf'

MEDIUM PURPLE
Lavandula angustifolia
'Buena Vista'

DARK PURPLE
Lavandula angustifolia
'Hidcote'

VIOLET
Lavandula angustifolia
'Folgate'

DARK VIOLET
Lavandula angustifolia
'Violet Intrigue'

LIGHT BLUE
Lavandula angustifolia
'Cedar Blue'

MEDIUM BLUE
Lavandula angustifolia
'Gray Lady'

RED
Lavandula stoechas
'Cottage Rose'

PLUM
Lavandula stoechas
'Helmsdale'

BICOLOR
Lavandula stoechas
'Ballerina'

The two red lavenders in this book both happen to be bicolor as well.

Foliage Color Guide

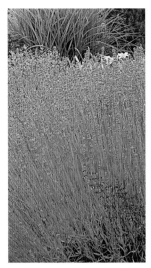

LIGHT GREEN
Lavandula ×intermedia
'Provence' (foreground)

GREEN
Lavandula angustifolia
'Blue Cushion'

MOSS GREEN
Lavandula stoechas
'Sugarberry Ruffles'

GRAY-GREEN
Lavandula ×intermedia
'Alba'

SILVER
Lavandula ×chaytorae
'Richard Gray'

The foliage color classification is based on plants during the summer months; during the winter, when plants are dormant, foliage color will change and become darker or duller, depending on the type of lavender.

Stem Length

The stems of a lavender plant can range from short (3–6 inches) to very long (16–18 inches) and any length in between. Angustifolia varieties usually have shorter stems than lavandins, yet some angustifolias have stems up to 12 inches long, making them desirable to clip as fresh cut flowers. The botanical term used to describe the stem, which sprouts from the foliage and ends where the flowers of the lavender begin, is peduncle. Peduncles can grow more upright or have a wavy appearance. For the sake of simplicity, I describe only the stem length here, not peduncle characteristics.

Bloom Frequency and Timing

Lavenders can bloom once, twice, or several times in a season, depending on how long the summer lasts and how soon the flowers are harvested. Each entry in the lavender palette tells you how many times the plant blooms and when it begins blooming. Plants characterized as blooming once can produce a smaller second or even a third bloom in one season if the flowers are cut soon enough. Plants characterized as blooming twice have been known to produce a full second flush after the flowers from the first bloom have been harvested. Plants characterized as blooming continuously will produce several full flowerings in a season if the flowers are removed after each flush. Areas with warmer weather can have longer seasons and a greater number of blooms in a season.

Exactly when your plant blooms depends on the weather, but generally a particular variety will start to bloom about the same time each year. Angustifolias vary more than some other species as to when they begin to flower. Lavenders listed in the lavender palette as blooming in early spring blossom first in the season; in my garden, that usually means the first part of May to mid-May if the weather cooperates. Spring bloomers are the next to flower, which means around the end of May to the first part of June for my plants. Lavenders characterized as late spring bloomers begin their bloom cycle through the month of June where I live. Early summer bloomers are those that start here in July. Depending on where you live, spring may arrive sooner or later than where I live, but the sequence of blooms from early spring through early summer still holds true.

Plant Height and Spacing

The plant height given in each entry in the lavender palette is based on how high a plant can be expected to grow by year three if it has been trimmed properly from the beginning. Lavender is considered full grown by year three but will continue to grow until year five, so keep that in mind when spacing your lavender plants. The range of sizes given takes into account different climates and growing conditions, as do the spacing suggestions.

Hardiness and Climate Zones

There are several factors to think about when you are determining which varieties of lavender will thrive where you live. The first is hardiness. The plant hardiness zone temperature chart put out by the U.S. Department of Agriculture names eleven zones based on lowest average temperatures. For example, if a plant is rated hardy in zones 5–9, the plant can survive minimum temperatures ranging anywhere from −20 degrees F (the lowest temperature in zone 5) to 30 degrees F (the highest low temperature in zone 9). The best way to determine your temperature zone is to find out the historical lowest winter temperature in your area and locate it on the temperature chart. Then look for lavenders that are rated hardy in this zone.

But using minimum temperatures as a guide is only part of the equation. For example, Portland, Oregon, and Austin, Texas, are in the same temperature zone but their climates are very different. Portland gets significantly more rainfall, and Austin has much higher humidity in the summer. These climate conditions can have a big impact on whether lavender will thrive and which types of lavender can grow in your area. Temperature highs, sun exposure, humidity levels, wind, and soil type are also important factors to consider in choosing the right lavender for your area.

Sunset magazine has prepared climate zone maps for the entire United States that take into account not only temperatures but also factors such as amount of rainfall, length of growing season, latitude, elevation, and ocean influence. To find your *Sunset* climate zone and corresponding recommended plant species, go to www.sunset.com/garden/climate-zones. These maps can be a useful tool when considering whether your area is right for growing a particular plant.

With that said about temperature and climate zones, keep in mind that your individual plot may not have the same overall growing characteristics as your region as a whole. For this reason, I recommend that you determine the microclimates in your yard and choose plants suited to the temperature zone these represent.

Plant Hardiness Zones

Here are the average annual minimum temperatures for plant hardiness zones referred to in this chapter:

Zone	Temperature in °F	Temperature in °C
1	below −50	below −46
2	−50 to −40	−46 to −40
3	−40 to −30	−40 to −34
4	−30 to −20	−34 to −29
5	−20 to −10	−29 to −23
6	−10 to 0	−23 to −18
7	0 to 10	−18 to −12
8	10 to 20	−12 to −7
9	20 to 30	−7 to −1
10	30 to 40	−1 to 4
11	above 40	above 4

Where to Find These Lavenders

When you shop for lavenders, keep in mind that the source matters. How many times have you bought a plant at the local garden center or grocery store only to find out after it blooms that the plant you bought is not the one on the tag? If you are an avid gardener, the chances are good. Why is that? A plant from conception to retail center can go through several channels before it ends up in your yard. Many starts are brought in from other countries and rooted on arrival. These starts may go from a facility overseas to a growing house, then to a retail center and ultimately to your garden. Changing hands that many times can lead to a greater chance of mislabeling, especially with varieties that look so much alike.

To make matters more complicated, many of the cultivars described in this book have not been made available to the general public on a large scale. *Lavandula angustifolia* varieties such as 'Hidcote' and 'Munstead' are recommended on gardening websites as "the one to try," but these varieties are so often grown from seed that these strains most likely vary across the country. If having a lavender variety that is true to species is important to you, buying from a reputable breeder is the answer.

The movement toward sustainable agriculture and family farms has gained momentum over the last decade. Local growers who specialize in a particular type of plant generally have the knowledge to identify and produce plants that are true to variety. Even though any breeder can make mistakes, the likelihood of acquiring a mislabeled plant is minimized when you buy from nurseries that do their own propagating or garden centers that buy plants from local breeders.

At The Cutting Garden, Sequim, Washington

Lavandula ×allardii

Lavandula ×allardii

This tender lavender is a hybrid of *Lavandula dentata* and *L. latifolia*. The combination of soft silver foliage and long stems makes it a wonderful choice for gardeners in warmer climates, but it has a hard time making it through the winter in colder zones.

ORIGIN: native to the Mediterranean
FLOWER COLOR: light purple
FOLIAGE COLOR: gray-green
STEM LENGTH: 14–18 inches
BLOOMS: once in early summer
PLANT HEIGHT: 30–36 inches
SPACING: 36 inches
HARDINESS: zones 8–10

This variety is best suited for areas that are frost-free. If you like its characteristics and would like to grow something similar, try *Lavandula ×chaytorae* varieties. These have proven to be hardier in areas that are colder in the winter.

Lavandula angustifolia

Lavandula angustifolia, sometimes called true or common lavender, is the most cold-hardy species of lavender. It is rated as hardy to zone 5, although some claim to be able to grow it in climates as cool as zone 4 or even 3. True lavenders are grown all over the world, in various climates, for their prized essential oil and beauty in the garden. Their fragrance is generally sweeter than that of other species, making them a great choice for culinary use. A spectrum of bloom color among individual cultivars may include blues, purples, violets, pinks, and even whites. Some are smaller or dwarf varieties, making them great for containers, while others can grow much larger, making them a good choice for a border or hedge. The flowers of *L. angustifolia* tend to be more vibrant than those of other species. Some have short stems; others may have peduncles up to 15 inches long.

True lavenders need to be grown in locations where they can go dormant during the winter months. In areas of high rainfall, extra care needs to be taken to ensure they get proper drainage. Snow can actually benefit the plants during the winter by providing insulation. Angustifolias can be prone to sudden wilts in areas of high humidity in the summertime. However, microclimates vary significantly, so you may have success depending on your individual area. To date, no extensive studies have been done to determine which angustifolias can survive in more humid conditions, so trial and error may your best bet.

Lavandula angustifolia 'Seal's Seven Oaks' (left) and 'Tucker's Early' (right) at Joy Creek Nursery

Lavandula angustifolia 'Betty's Blue'

✳ 'Betty's Blue'

ORIGIN: Nichols Garden Nursery, Albany, Oregon, 1998
FLOWER COLOR: dark blue
FOLIAGE COLOR: gray-green
STEM LENGTH: 6–8 inches
BLOOMS: once in early summer
PLANT HEIGHT: 30 inches
SPACING: 30–36 inches
HARDINESS: zones 5–9

❧ 'Betty's Blue' is a great choice for crafts because of its deep blue color and tight flower heads.

 indicates Sarah's top picks.

Lavandula angustifolia 'Blue Cushion'

'Blue Cushion'
also sold as 'Schola'

ORIGIN: Blooms of Bressingham, Suffolk, England, 1992
FLOWER COLOR: light blue
FOLIAGE COLOR: green
STEM LENGTH: 8–10 inches
BLOOMS: once in spring
PLANT HEIGHT: 18–24 inches
SPACING: 24 inches
HARDINESS: zones 5–9

❧ This is a compact variety that would do well in a container.

Lavandula angustifolia 'Blue River'

Lavandula angustifolia 'Bowles Early'

'Blue River'

ORIGIN: a seed strain from Holland, year unknown
FLOWER COLOR: dark purple
FOLIAGE COLOR: green
STEM LENGTH: 6–8 inches
BLOOMS: once in early summer
PLANT HEIGHT: 12–20 inches
SPACING: 24 inches
HARDINESS: zones 5-9

The flower heads on 'Blue River' are tight and compact. If you look into the flower heads closely, you will see tiny specks of orange.

'Bowles Early'

ORIGIN: Hardy Plant Farm, Middlesex, England, 1913
FLOWER COLOR: medium purple
FOLIAGE COLOR: gray-green
STEM LENGTH: 8–10 inches
BLOOMS: once in spring
PLANT HEIGHT: 24–30 inches
SPACING: 30 inches
HARDINESS: zones 5-9

'Bowles Early' received the award of merit from the Royal Horticultural Society in 1963.

Lavandula angustifolia 'Brabant Blue'

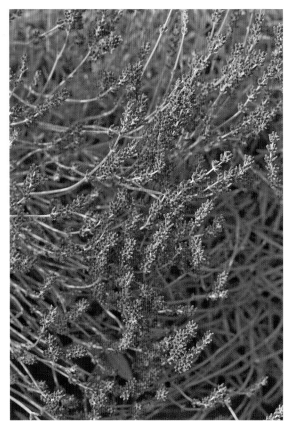

Lavandula angustifolia 'Buena Vista'

'Brabant Blue'

ORIGIN: unknown
FLOWER COLOR: light blue
FOLIAGE COLOR: gray-green
STEM LENGTH: 12–14 inches
BLOOMS: once in late spring
PLANT HEIGHT: 30–36 inches
SPACING: 36 inches
HARDINESS: zones 5–9

🌢 'Brabant Blue' is a great choice for culinary purposes thanks to its exceptionally sweet fragrance.

✳ 'Buena Vista'

ORIGIN: Donald Roberts, Premier Botanicals, Independence, Oregon, 1981
FLOWER COLOR: medium purple
FOLIAGE COLOR: green
STEM LENGTH: 10–12 inches
BLOOMS: continuously starting in spring
PLANT HEIGHT: 24–30 inches
SPACING: 30 inches
HARDINESS: zones 5–9

🌢 'Buena Vista' is sought after for its sweet fragrance. This continuous bloomer will blanket your garden in lavender all summer and is a good choice for culinary use.

Lavandula angustifolia 'Cedar Blue'

'Cedar Blue'

ORIGIN: Muntons Microplants, Suffolk, England, 1995
FLOWER COLOR: light blue
FOLIAGE COLOR: green
STEM LENGTH: 10–12 inches
BLOOMS: once in spring
PLANT HEIGHT: 30 inches
SPACING: 30–36 inches
HARDINESS: zones 5–9

🌿 'Cedar Blue' has beautiful long-lasting blue flowers.

Lavandula angustifolia 'Coconut Ice'

'Coconut Ice'

ORIGIN: Virginia McNaughton, Lavender Downs, West Melton, New Zealand, 1997
FLOWER COLOR: pink
FOLIAGE COLOR: gray-green
STEM LENGTH: 10–12 inches
BLOOMS: once in spring
PLANT HEIGHT: 24–30 inches
SPACING: 30–36 inches
HARDINESS: zones 5–9

🌿 'Coconut Ice' produces both pink and white flowers on the same flower head, similar to 'Melissa'; however, the pink flowers are a bit darker.

Lavandula angustifolia 'Croxton's Wild'

Lavandula angustifolia 'Dark Supreme'

'Croxton's Wild'

ORIGIN: Thomas DeBaggio, Arlington, Virginia, via Pauline Croxton, 1994
FLOWER COLOR: violet
FOLIAGE COLOR: green
STEM LENGTH: 10–12 inches
BLOOMS: twice starting in early spring
PLANT HEIGHT: 30 inches
SPACING: 30–36 inches
HARDINESS: zones 5–9

🌢 This is one of the first lavenders to bloom in the spring. The blossoms appear white when opening, eventually changing to bright violet.

'Dark Supreme'
also sold as 'W. K. Doyle'

ORIGIN: Thomas DeBaggio, Arlington, Virginia, 1987
FLOWER COLOR: violet
FOLIAGE COLOR: gray-green
STEM LENGTH: 8–10 inches
BLOOMS: twice starting in early summer
PLANT HEIGHT: 24–30 inches
SPACING: 30–36 inches
HARDINESS: zones 5–9

🌢 The name 'Dark Supreme' implies a dark-flowering lavender, but this variety has a light violet flower color.

Lavandula angustifolia 'Dwarf Blue'

Lavandula angustifolia 'Faire Pink'

'Dwarf Blue'

ORIGIN: Amsterdam, 1911
FLOWER COLOR: light blue
FOLIAGE COLOR: gray-green
STEM LENGTH: 6–8 inches
BLOOMS: twice starting in spring
PLANT HEIGHT: 12–15 inches
SPACING: 15–20 inches
HARDINESS: zones 5–9

●◆ 'Dwarf Blue' has many names, including 'Baby Blue' and 'Nana'. This is a compact variety ideal for containers.

'Faire Pink'

ORIGIN: Faire Gardens, Tumwater, Washington, year unknown
FLOWER COLOR: pink
FOLIAGE COLOR: green
STEM LENGTH: 6–8 inches
BLOOMS: once in spring
PLANT HEIGHT: 24–30 inches
SPACING: 30 inches
HARDINESS: zones 5–9

●◆ 'Faire Pink' has a compact habit, making it a wonderful container plant.

Lavandula angustifolia 'Fiona English'

Lavandula angustifolia 'Folgate'

'Fiona English'

ORIGIN: Peter Carter, The Ploughman's Garden and Nursery, Waiuku, South Auckland, New Zealand, 1990
FLOWER COLOR: dark purple
FOLIAGE COLOR: gray-green
STEM LENGTH: 6–8 inches
BLOOMS: once in spring
PLANT HEIGHT: 30–36 inches
SPACING: 36 inches
HARDINESS: zones 5–9

•❖ The silver foliage contrasts beautifully with the dark purple blossoms of this plant.

❋ 'Folgate'

ORIGIN: Linn Chilvers, Norfolk, England, before 1933
FLOWER COLOR: light blue
FOLIAGE COLOR: gray-green
STEM LENGTH: 8–10 inches
BLOOMS: once in early spring
PLANT HEIGHT: 30 inches
SPACING: 30–36 inches
HARDINESS: zones 5–9

•❖ The flowers on 'Folgate' appear to be an almost iridescent periwinkle blue. 'Folgate' is known to be particularly hardy in colder climates.

Lavandula angustifolia 'French Fields'

Lavandula angustifolia 'Graves'

'French Fields'

ORIGIN: unknown
FLOWER COLOR: purple
FOLIAGE COLOR: green
STEM LENGTH: 8–10 inches
BLOOMS: continuously starting in spring
PLANT HEIGHT: 24–30 inches
SPACING: 30–36 inches
HARDINESS: zones 5–9

❧ 'French Fields' closely resembles lavender that appears to grow wild in the Mediterranean, hence the name.

'Graves'

ORIGIN: Tucker and Henson, 1985
FLOWER COLOR: medium purple
FOLIAGE COLOR: gray-green
STEM LENGTH: 8–10 inches
BLOOMS: once in spring
PLANT HEIGHT: 30–36 inches
SPACING: 36 inches
HARDINESS: zones 5–9

❧ 'Graves' tends to bloom for an extended period during the growing season.

Lavandula angustifolia 'Gray Lady'

Lavandula angustifolia 'Helen Batchelder'

'Gray Lady'

ORIGIN: Wayside Gardens, Mentor, Ohio, before 1967
FLOWER COLOR: medium purple
FOLIAGE COLOR: gray-green
STEM LENGTH: 6–8 inches
BLOOMS: once in late spring
PLANT HEIGHT: 30–36 inches
SPACING: 36 inches
HARDINESS: zones 5–9

✺ 'Gray Lady' is a fast grower with excellent form for beautiful bouquets.

'Helen Batchelder'

ORIGIN: named after Helen T. Batchelder of the New England Unit of the Herb Society of America, 1967
FLOWER COLOR: medium purple
FOLIAGE COLOR: green
STEM LENGTH: 6–8 inches
BLOOMS: once in spring
PLANT HEIGHT: 18–20 inches
SPACING: 24 inches
HARDINESS: zones 6–9

✺ 'Helen Batchelder' is a good choice for containers.

Lavandula angustifolia 'Hidcote'

Lavandula angustifolia 'Hidcote Pink'

'Hidcote'

ORIGIN: Hidcote Manor, France, early 1920s
FLOWER COLOR: dark blue
FOLIAGE COLOR: green
STEM LENGTH: 6–8 inches
BLOOMS: once in spring
PLANT HEIGHT: 12–20 inches
SPACING: 20–24 inches
HARDINESS: zones 5–9

The popularity of 'Hidcote' has led to several seed-raised plants that vary from the true form. This entry describes the true strain.

'Hidcote Pink'

ORIGIN: Major Lawrence Johnston, Hidcote Manor, Gloucester, England, before 1957 (Johnston brought Hidcote to England from France in the 1920s)
FLOWER COLOR: light pink
FOLIAGE COLOR: green
STEM LENGTH: 6–8 inches
BLOOMS: once in spring
PLANT HEIGHT: 30–36 inches
SPACING: 36 inches
HARDINESS: zones 5–9

'Hidcote Pink' has a strong, sweet fragrance and is great for culinary use.

Lavandula angustifolia 'Hidcote Superior'

'Hidcote Superior'

ORIGIN: Jelitto Perennial Seeds, Schwarmstedt, Germany, 2002
FLOWER COLOR: dark purple
FOLIAGE COLOR: green
STEM LENGTH: 6–8 inches
BLOOMS: once in spring
PLANT HEIGHT: 20–24 inches
SPACING: 24 inches
HARDINESS: zones 5–9

🌿 'Hidcote Superior' is one of the darkest-blooming lavenders.

Lavandula angustifolia 'Imperial Gem'

'Imperial Gem'

ORIGIN: Norfolk Lavender, Norfolk, England, 1960s
FLOWER COLOR: dark blue
FOLIAGE COLOR: gray-green
STEM LENGTH: 10–14 inches
BLOOMS: once in spring
PLANT HEIGHT: 24–30 inches
SPACING: 30–36 inches
HARDINESS: zones 5–9

🌿 'Imperial Gem' is similar to the true strain of 'Hidcote' but with larger flower heads.

Lavandula angustifolia 'Irene Doyle'

Lavandula angustifolia 'Lavenite Petite'

'Irene Doyle'
also sold as 'Two Seasons'

ORIGIN: Thomas DeBaggio, Arlington, Virginia, 1981
FLOWER COLOR: dark purple
FOLIAGE COLOR: gray-green
STEM LENGTH: 10–12 inches
BLOOMS: twice starting in early spring
PLANT HEIGHT: 24–30 inches
SPACING: 30–36 inches
HARDINESS: zones 5–9

➻ A prolific bloomer with a strong, desirable fragrance, this cultivar is also aptly named 'Two Seasons' because of its ability to produce two full blooms during the growing season.

'Lavenite Petite'

ORIGIN: Virginia McNaughton, Downderry Nursery, Kent, England, 1989
FLOWER COLOR: dark purple
FOLIAGE COLOR: gray-green
STEM LENGTH: 6–8 inches
BLOOMS: once in early spring
PLANT HEIGHT: 12–15 inches
SPACING: 15–24 inches
HARDINESS: zones 5–9

➻ 'Lavenite Petite' is a wonderful choice for container gardening thanks to its short, dark stems and tight foliage. This variety is patented.

Lavandula angustifolia 'Little Lottie'

Lavandula angustifolia 'Loddon Blue'

'Little Lottie'
also sold as 'Clarmo'

ORIGIN: Norfolk Lavender, Norfolk, England, 1998
FLOWER COLOR: light pink
FOLIAGE COLOR: gray-green
STEM LENGTH: 6–8 inches
BLOOMS: once in spring
PLANT HEIGHT: 20–24 inches
SPACING: 24–30 inches
HARDINESS: zones 5–9

❧ 'Little Lottie' is very fragrant and a great choice for culinary use.

'Loddon Blue'

ORIGIN: Thomas Carlile, Loddon Nurseries, Berkshire, England, 1959
FLOWER COLOR: medium violet
FOLIAGE COLOR: gray-green
STEM LENGTH: 8–10 inches
BLOOMS: once in early summer
PLANT HEIGHT: 30–36 inches
SPACING: 36–48 inches
HARDINESS: zones 5–9

❧ 'Loddon Blue' can be prone to wilts in humid climates during summer months.

Lavandula angustifolia 'Maillette'

Lavandula angustifolia 'Martha Roderick'

'Maillette'

ORIGIN: Monsieur Maillet, Valensole, France, before 1959
FLOWER COLOR: medium purple
FOLIAGE COLOR: gray-green
STEM LENGTH: 10–12 inches
BLOOMS: once in spring
PLANT HEIGHT: 24–30 inches
SPACING: 30–36 inches
HARDINESS: zones 5–9

➽ 'Maillette' is considered one of the best angustifolia varieties for oil distillation.

'Martha Roderick'

ORIGIN: M. Nevin Smith, Watsonville, California, 1981–82
FLOWER COLOR: medium purple
FOLIAGE COLOR: gray-green
STEM LENGTH: 6–8 inches
BLOOMS: once in early summer
PLANT HEIGHT: 24–30 inches
SPACING: 30–36 inches
HARDINESS: zones 5–9

➽ 'Martha Roderick' has a sweet floral fragrance, great for bouquets or dried bunches.

Lavandula angustifolia 'Melissa'

✳ 'Melissa'

ORIGIN: Van Hevelingen Herb Nursery, Newburg, Oregon, 1994
FLOWER COLOR: light pink
FOLIAGE COLOR: green
STEM LENGTH: 8–10 inches
BLOOMS: once in early summer
PLANT HEIGHT: 30 inches
SPACING: 30–36 inches
HARDINESS: zones 5–9

☙ 'Melissa' is often used for culinary purposes. Some describe it as having a peppery hint, making it a good choice for savory dishes.

Lavandula angustifolia 'Miss Katherine'

Lavandula angustifolia 'Mitcham Gray'

'Miss Katherine'

ORIGIN: Norfolk Lavender, Norfolk, England, 1992
FLOWER COLOR: pink
FOLIAGE COLOR: green
STEM LENGTH: 12–14 inches
BLOOMS: once in spring
PLANT HEIGHT: 24–30 inches
SPACING: 30–36 inches
HARDINESS: zones 5–9

❧ This is one of the darkest-flowering pink varieties of lavender.

'Mitcham Gray'

ORIGIN: exact origin unknown but could possibly have originated as 'Nana Atropurpurea' and then been selected as a cultivar on its own, before 1978
FLOWER COLOR: medium purple
FOLIAGE COLOR: gray
STEM LENGTH: 6–8 inches
BLOOMS: once in late spring
PLANT HEIGHT: 30–36 inches
SPACING: 36 inches
HARDINESS: zones 5–9

❧ This variety is similar to 'Munstead'.

Lavandula angustifolia 'Munstead'

'Munstead'

ORIGIN: Gertrude Jekyll, Munstead Wood, West Surrey, England, 1902
FLOWER COLOR: medium purple
FOLIAGE COLOR: gray-green
STEM LENGTH: 6–8 inches
BLOOMS: twice starting in spring
PLANT HEIGHT: 20–24 inches
SPACING: 24–30 inches
HARDINESS: zones 5–9

Growers have raised this variety, which has become synonymous with true lavender, from seed so often that variations have shown up widely. The true strain is pictured here.

Lavandula angustifolia 'Nana Atropurpurea'

'Nana Atropurpurea'

ORIGIN: unknown
FLOWER COLOR: dark purple
FOLIAGE COLOR: gray-green
STEM LENGTH: 6–8 inches
BLOOMS: once in spring
PLANT HEIGHT: 18–20 inches
SPACING: 20–24 inches
HARDINESS: zones 5–9

❧ This variety is listed in many plant catalogs as a cultivar of *Lavandula* ×*intermedia*.

Lavandula angustifolia 'Peter Pan'

'Peter Pan'

ORIGIN: Simon Charlesworth, Downderry Nursery, Kent, England, 2001
FLOWER COLOR: dark purple
FOLIAGE COLOR: gray-green
STEM LENGTH: 10–12 inches
BLOOMS: once in late spring
PLANT HEIGHT: 20–24 inches
SPACING: 24–30 inches
HARDINESS: zones 5–9

❧ This variety is a dark bloomer similar to 'Hidcote'.

Lavandula angustifolia 'Premier'

'Premier'

ORIGIN: Donald Roberts, Premier Botanicals, Independence, Oregon, 1990
FLOWER COLOR: medium purple
FOLIAGE COLOR: green
STEM LENGTH: 10–12 inches
BLOOMS: twice starting in late spring
PLANT HEIGHT: 24–30 inches
SPACING: 30–36 inches
HARDINESS: zones 5–9

❧ 'Premier' has a light, sweet fragrance.

Lavandula angustifolia 'Princess Blue'

'Princess Blue'

ORIGIN: Norfolk Lavender, Norfolk, England, early 1960s
FLOWER COLOR: medium violet
FOLIAGE COLOR: gray-green
STEM LENGTH: 10–12 inches
BLOOMS: once in spring
PLANT HEIGHT: 30–36 inches
SPACING: 36 inches
HARDINESS: zones 5–9

❧ 'Princess Blue' has been confused in the nursery trade with 'Nana', sometimes referred to as 'Nana 2'.

Lavandula angustifolia 'Purple Bouquet'

Lavandula angustifolia 'Rosea'

✳ 'Purple Bouquet'

ORIGIN: Sunshine Herb Farm, Tenino, Washington, 2006
FLOWER COLOR: dark purple
FOLIAGE COLOR: gray-green
STEM LENGTH: 12–15 inches
BLOOMS: twice starting in early summer
PLANT HEIGHT: 24–30 inches
SPACING: 30–36 inches
HARDINESS: zones 5–9

🍃 The long, dark stems of 'Purple Bouquet' make it a good choice for bouquets or crafts.

'Rosea'
also sold as 'Jean Davis'

ORIGIN: England, before 1937
FLOWER COLOR: pink
FOLIAGE COLOR: green
STEM LENGTH: 6–8 inches
BLOOMS: once in spring
PLANT HEIGHT: 24–30 inches
SPACING: 30–36 inches
HARDINESS: zones 5–9

🍃 'Rosea' is more commonly labeled in the United States as 'Jean Davis'; the origin of this name is not known.

Lavandula angustifolia 'Royal Purple'

✳ 'Royal Purple'

ORIGIN: Norfolk Lavender, Norfolk, England, 1944
FLOWER COLOR: light violet
FOLIAGE COLOR: green
STEM LENGTH: 12–14 inches
BLOOMS: once in late spring
PLANT HEIGHT: 30–36 inches
SPACING: 36–42 inches
HARDINESS: zones 5–9

🖙 This very large angustifolia variety makes a good choice for hedging.

Lavandula angustifolia 'Royal Velvet'

Lavandula angustifolia 'Sachet'

✳ 'Royal Velvet'

ORIGIN: Van Hevelingen Herb Nursery, Newburg, Oregon, 1980s
FLOWER COLOR: dark blue
FOLIAGE COLOR: gray-green
STEM LENGTH: 12–14 inches
BLOOMS: twice starting in spring
PLANT HEIGHT: 24–30 inches
SPACING: 30–36 inches
HARDINESS: zones 5–9

🌬 'Royal Velvet' is one of the best varieties for fresh or dried bouquets.

'Sachet'

ORIGIN: Donald Roberts, Premier Botanicals, Independence, Oregon, 1988
FLOWER COLOR: medium purple
FOLIAGE COLOR: gray-green
STEM LENGTH: 6–8 inches
BLOOMS: twice starting in spring
PLANT HEIGHT: 24–30 inches
SPACING: 30–36 inches
HARDINESS: zones 5–9

🌬 This variety has a wonderful fragrance and is great for sachets, hence the name.

Lavandula angustifolia 'Sarah'

'Sarah'

ORIGIN: California, late 1980s
FLOWER COLOR: medium purple
FOLIAGE COLOR: green
STEM LENGTH: 6–8 inches
BLOOMS: twice starting in late spring
PLANT HEIGHT: 20–24 inches
SPACING: 24–30 inches
HARDINESS: zones 6–9

This variety is a slow starter, but by the second year 'Sarah' smothers itself in flowers.

Lavandula angustifolia 'Seal's Seven Oaks'

'Seal's Seven Oaks'

ORIGIN: The Herb Farm, Seal, Kent, England, 1980s
FLOWER COLOR: medium violet
FOLIAGE COLOR: green
STEM LENGTH: 12–14 inches
BLOOMS: twice starting in early spring
PLANT HEIGHT: 30–36 inches
SPACING: 36–48 inches
HARDINESS: zones 5–9

This variety is one of the first lavenders to bloom in the spring.

Lavandula angustifolia 'Sharon Roberts'

Lavandula angustifolia 'Sleeping Beauty'

'Sharon Roberts'

ORIGIN: Donald Roberts, Premier Botanicals, Independence, Oregon, 1989
FLOWER COLOR: medium purple
FOLIAGE COLOR: green
STEM LENGTH: 12–14 inches
BLOOMS: continuously starting in spring
PLANT HEIGHT: 24–30 inches
SPACING: 30–36 inches
HARDINESS: zones 5–9

This variety, which Donald Roberts named after his wife, is very similar to 'Buena Vista' but with slightly darker blossoms.

'Sleeping Beauty'
also sold as 'Carolyn Dille'

ORIGIN: Thomas DeBaggio, Arlington, Virginia, 1988
FLOWER COLOR: medium purple
FOLIAGE COLOR: green
STEM LENGTH: 10–12 inches
BLOOMS: once in spring
PLANT HEIGHT: 24–30 inches
SPACING: 30–36 inches
HARDINESS: zones 5–9

'Sleeping Beauty' is a slow grower but produces beautiful blue flowers on short, wavy stems.

Lavandula angustifolia 'Thumbelina Leigh'

Lavandula angustifolia 'Tucker's Early Purple'

'Thumbelina Leigh'

ORIGIN: Elsie and Brian Hall, Blenheim, New Zealand, mid-1990s
FLOWER COLOR: dark violet
FOLIAGE COLOR: green
STEM LENGTH: 4–6 inches
BLOOMS: once in late spring
PLANT HEIGHT: 20–24 inches
SPACING: 24–30 inches
HARDINESS: zones 5–9

🌿 Its compact growth habit and short spikes make this variety great for containers. Propagation for commercial purposes is prohibited as it is patented.

'Tucker's Early Purple'

ORIGIN: Thomas DeBaggio, Arlington, Virginia, 1993
FLOWER COLOR: medium purple
FOLIAGE COLOR: green
STEM LENGTH: 4–6 inches
BLOOMS: continuously starting in early spring
PLANT HEIGHT: 18–24 inches
SPACING: 24–30 inches
HARDINESS: zones 5–9

🌿 This is a great container variety because of its compact size and frequency of blooms.

Lavandula angustifolia 'Twickel Purple'

'Twickel Purple'

ORIGIN: Kasteel Twickel, Holland, before 1922
FLOWER COLOR: medium purple
FOLIAGE COLOR: gray-green
STEM LENGTH: 10–12 inches
BLOOMS: once in late spring
PLANT HEIGHT: 30–40 inches
SPACING: 36–48 inches
HARDINESS: zones 5–9

There is also a Twickel Purple group that includes longer-stemmed angustifolias such as 'Royal Purple' and 'Royal Velvet'.

Lavandula angustifolia 'Victorian Amethyst'

'Victorian Amethyst'

ORIGIN: from Canada, raised by Barbara Remington, Dutch Mill Herb Farm, Forest Grove, Oregon, 1980s
FLOWER COLOR: dark blue
FOLIAGE COLOR: gray-green
STEM LENGTH: 6–8 inches
BLOOMS: once in spring
PLANT HEIGHT: 20–24 inches
SPACING: 24–30 inches
HARDINESS: zones 5–9

This variety offers a stunning array of deep blue to purple flowers.

Lavandula angustifolia 'Violet Intrigue'

'Violet Intrigue'

ORIGIN: Virginia McNaughton and Dennis
 Matthews, Christchurch, New Zealand, 2002
FLOWER COLOR: dark violet
FOLIAGE COLOR: gray-green
STEM LENGTH: 10–12 inches
BLOOMS: once in spring
PLANT HEIGHT: 30–36 inches
SPACING: 36 inches
HARDINESS: zones 5–9

●◆ This patented variety is prized for its exceptional bloom quality and habit.

Lavandula angustifolia 'Wyckoff'

'Wyckoff'
also sold as 'Wyckoff Blue'

ORIGIN: L. J. Wyckoff, Seattle, Washington,
 before 1951
FLOWER COLOR: medium purple
FOLIAGE COLOR: gray-green
STEM LENGTH: 6–8 inches
BLOOMS: once in early summer
PLANT HEIGHT: 30–36 inches
SPACING: 36 inches
HARDINESS: zones 5–9

●◆ This cultivar produces beautiful flowers but is
difficult to grow.

Lavandula ×chaytorae 'Ana Luisa'

Lavandula ×chaytorae

These lavender crosses are so great that you should have one (or two or three) in your garden. They are truly stunning and make a wonderful addition to just about any growing space. They combine the silvery, fuzzy foliage of *Lavandula lanata* or woolly lavender with the vibrant blossoms and hardiness of *L. angustifolia*. The silver foliage looks good all winter, making it a striking hedging plant. The spikes usually have a silvery hint, complementing the foliage with light purple to medium purple flower heads. They have a gentle, sweet fragrance, and longer-stemmed varieties are a good pick for lavender wands. Whether they can survive brutal winters for extended periods of time has been virtually untested, but positive reports of survival rates in temperatures as low as −10 degrees F have been made.

✳ 'Ana Luisa'

ORIGIN: Van Hevelingen Herb Nursery, Newburg, Oregon, 1998
FLOWER COLOR: dark purple
FOLIAGE COLOR: silver
STEM LENGTH: 20–25 inches
BLOOMS: once in early summer
PLANT HEIGHT: 36–42 inches
SPACING: 36–48 inches
HARDINESS: zones 7–10

This is one of the largest varieties of this species, with long stems that bloom in a rounded shape.

Lavandula ×chaytorae 'Andreas'

Lavandula ×chaytorae 'Jennifer'

'Andreas'

ORIGIN: New Zealand, early 1990s
FLOWER COLOR: dark violet
FOLIAGE COLOR: silver
STEM LENGTH: 4–6 inches
BLOOMS: once in early summer
PLANT HEIGHT: 30–36 inches
SPACING: 36–42 inches
HARDINESS: zones 7–10

● 'Andreas' produces the shortest stems of any *Lavandula ×chaytorae* variety and needs a hard pruning to keep its shape.

'Jennifer'

ORIGIN: Van Hevelingen Herb Nursery, Newburg, Oregon, 2001
FLOWER COLOR: dark purple
FOLIAGE COLOR: silver
STEM LENGTH: 12–14 inches
BLOOMS: once in early summer
PLANT HEIGHT: 32–36 inches
SPACING: 36 inches
HARDINESS: zones 7–10

● The blue-violet flowers of Jennifer are lighter in color than those of 'Lisa Marie' and held in larger flower heads.

Lavandula ×chaytorae 'Joan Head'

Lavandula ×chaytorae 'Kathleen Elizabeth'

'Joan Head'

ORIGIN: Peter Carter, The Ploughman's Garden and Nursery, Waiuku, South Auckland, New Zealand, mid-1990s
FLOWER COLOR: dark violet
FOLIAGE COLOR: silver
STEM LENGTH: 15–20 inches
BLOOMS: once in early summer
PLANT HEIGHT: 40–48 inches
SPACING: at least 48 inches
HARDINESS: zones 7–10

🖙 This variety is named after Joan Head, editor of *The Lavender Bag*, an international newsletter for lavender enthusiasts published in England.

'Kathleen Elizabeth'
also sold as 'Silver Frost'

ORIGIN: Van Hevelingen Herb Nursery, Newburg, Oregon, 1991
FLOWER COLOR: violet
FOLIAGE COLOR: silver
STEM LENGTH: 12–14 inches
BLOOMS: once in early summer
PLANT HEIGHT: 36–48 inches
SPACING: 48 inches
HARDINESS: zones 7–10

🖙 This cross between *Lavandula lanata* and *L. angustifolia* produces dark violet flowers, and the soft silver foliage holds its color all year, making it a wonderful landscape plant.

Lavandula ×chaytorae 'Lisa Marie'

Lavandula ×chaytorae 'Richard Gray'

'Lisa Marie'

ORIGIN: Kenneth R. Montgomery, Anderson Valley Nursery, Boonville, California, 1991
FLOWER COLOR: dark blue
FOLIAGE COLOR: silver
STEM LENGTH: 10–14 inches
BLOOMS: once in early summer
PLANT HEIGHT: 24–30 inches
SPACING: 30–36 inches
HARDINESS: zones 6–9

❧ This cross between *Lavandula angustifolia* 'Martha Roderick' and *L. lanata* is one of the more compact varieties of this species.

'Richard Gray'

ORIGIN: Royal Botanic Gardens, Kew, mid-1980s
FLOWER COLOR: medium purple
FOLIAGE COLOR: silver
STEM LENGTH: 10–12 inches
BLOOMS: once in early summer
PLANT HEIGHT: 36–40 inches
SPACING: 40–42 inches
HARDINESS: zones 6–9

❧ 'Richard Gray' has shorter spikes and tighter foliage than other cultivars in the same species.

Lavandula dentata 'Linda Ligon'

Lavandula dentata

The leaves of this lavender are coarse-toothed or dentate, and thus its name. The species is tender and should be protected during the winter months (or can be considered an annual in colder climates), making it a great choice for large pots and window boxes that can easily be covered. The plant has a fragrance that resembles eucalyptus.

'Linda Ligon'

ORIGIN: Thomas DeBaggio, Arlington, Virginia, 1980
FLOWER COLOR: light violet
FOLIAGE COLOR: variegated
STEM LENGTH: 6–8 inches
BLOOMS: continuously starting in spring
PLANT HEIGHT: 24–30 inches
SPACING: 30 inches
HARDINESS: zones 8–10

This unique lavender has bright green foliage with creamy variegation. If you want to propagate it from cuttings, it is important to include variegation in the cutting material; otherwise the new plant will revert to green only.

Lavandula ×*ginginsii* 'Goodwin Creek'

Lavandula ×*ginginsii*

This hybrid is a cross between *Lavandula dentata* (toothed lavender) and *L. lanata* (woolly lavender). The only selection to date, 'Goodwin Creek', produces woolly silver-gray foliage that thrives in warmer climates. This tender lavender should be protected during the winter months.

'Goodwin Creek'

ORIGIN: Jim Becker, Goodwin Creek Gardens, Williams, Oregon, 1991
FLOWER COLOR: purple
FOLIAGE COLOR: silver-gray
STEM LENGTH: 6–8 inches
BLOOMS: continuously starting in spring
PLANT HEIGHT: 30–36 inches
SPACING: 36 inches
HARDINESS: zones 8–10

➥ 'Goodwin Creek' needs winter protection during colder months. This variety grows well in more humid climates.

Lavandula ×intermedia

Lavandula ×intermedia varieties, or lavandins, are a cross between *L. angustifolia* and *L. latifolia* (spiked lavender). They tend to grow larger, bloom later, and produce more spikes than other lavenders. Their fragrance has a distinctive camphoric note, which means the oil has a somewhat woody undertone. Lavandins are the most widely distilled lavender, mainly because their oil yield can be up to five times that of *L. angustifolia* varieties. They make a beautiful show in a garden and are a great choice for hedging, as they can grow to 48 inches high or higher and produce long spikes up to 30 inches. In recent years, new varieties have blessed us with darker, more vibrant blooms, and there are even two white cultivars. One variety included here, 'Silver Edge', is variegated. Most *Lavandula ×intermedia* varieties are hardy to zone 5. They are resistant to certain types of fungal diseases in hot, humid climates.

Lavender with coreopsis and lamb's ear

Lavandula ×intermedia 'Alba'

Lavandula ×intermedia 'Dilly Dilly'

'Alba'
also sold as 'Dutch White' or 'Grosso White'

ORIGIN: possibly from The Herb Farm, Seal, Kent, England, 1930s
FLOWER COLOR: white
FOLIAGE COLOR: gray-green
STEM LENGTH: 25–30 inches
BLOOMS: once in early summer
PLANT HEIGHT: 48–52 inches
SPACING: 60 inches
HARDINESS: zones 5–9

The flowers of 'Alba' are a creamy white in comparison to the bright white blossoms of 'Edelweiss'.

'Dilly Dilly'

ORIGIN: unknown
FLOWER COLOR: medium purple
FOLIAGE COLOR: gray-green
STEM LENGTH: 12–14 inches
BLOOMS: once in early summer
PLANT HEIGHT: 30–36 inches
SPACING: 36 inches
HARDINESS: zones 5–9

This variety is very similar to 'Fat Spike' but the plants are smaller.

Lavandula ×intermedia 'Edelweiss'

'Edelweiss'

ORIGIN: possibly from The Herb Farm, Seal, Kent, England, 1960s
FLOWER COLOR: white
FOLIAGE COLOR: gray-green
STEM LENGTH: 18–24 inches
BLOOMS: once in early summer
PLANT HEIGHT: 24–30 inches
SPACING: 30–36 inches
HARDINESS: zones 5–9

☙ With bright white flowers, 'Edelweiss' has a habit similar to 'Grosso' and has sometimes been referred to as 'Grosso White'. If you look at the flower spikes closely, they have a hint of blue along the calyxes or flower buds. 'Edelweiss' has also been called 'Caty Blanc' in the trade, but 'Caty Blanc' is different in that the calyxes have a pink instead of blue tint.

Lavandula ×intermedia 'Fat Spike'

Lavandula ×intermedia 'Fragrant Memories'

'Fat Spike'
also sold as 'Fat Spike Grosso'

ORIGIN: Art Tucker, DeBaggio Nursery, Arlington, Virginia, early 1980s
FLOWER COLOR: light purple
FOLIAGE COLOR: gray-green
STEM LENGTH: 16–20 inches
BLOOMS: twice starting in early summer
PLANT HEIGHT: 36–42 inches
SPACING: 42 inches
HARDINESS: zones 5–9

🌿 'Fat Spike' is a great choice for wands and sachets. The flower buds are packed with oil, and the fragrance lasts a long time.

'Fragrant Memories'

ORIGIN: Blooms of Bressingham, Suffolk, England, 1984
FLOWER COLOR: light purple
FOLIAGE COLOR: silver
STEM LENGTH: 20–24 inches
BLOOMS: once in early summer
PLANT HEIGHT: 36–42 inches
SPACING: 42 inches
HARDINESS: zones 5–9

🌿 Its silver foliage and large size make 'Fragrant Memories' a great choice for hedging.

Lavandula ×intermedia 'Fred Boutin'

'Fred Boutin'

ORIGIN: M. N. Smith, Wintergreen Wholesale Nursery, Watsonville, CA, 1984
FLOWER COLOR: light purple
FOLIAGE COLOR: silver
STEM LENGTH: 16–18 inches
BLOOMS: once in summer
PLANT HEIGHT: 36–48 inches
SPACING: 48 inches
HARDINESS: zones 5–9

 'Fred Boutin' is one of the last to bloom in the season. It forms a large hedge when planted in a row.

Lavandula ×intermedia 'Grappenhall'

Lavandula ×intermedia 'Gros Bleu'

'Grappenhall'
also sold as 'Pale Pretender'

ORIGIN: Clibrans Ltd., Altrincham, Trafford, England, year unknown
FLOWER COLOR: light purple
FOLIAGE COLOR: gray-green
STEM LENGTH: 18–20 inches
BLOOMS: once in early summer
PLANT HEIGHT: 48–56 inches
SPACING: 60 inches
HARDINESS: zones 5–9

꒰ 'Grappenhall' is an example of a lavender that has been overpropagated, and the original variety is difficult to identify. It is known for a large bloom habit with typical long lavandin stems, making it a good choice for hedging.

✳ 'Gros Bleu'

ORIGIN: possibly from the Chambre d'Agriculture farm, Mevouillon, France, year unknown
FLOWER COLOR: dark blue
FOLIAGE COLOR: gray-green
STEM LENGTH: 18–20 inches
BLOOMS: once in early summer
PLANT HEIGHT: 36–40 inches
SPACING: 36–48 inches
HARDINESS: zones 5–9

꒰ The flower spikes of 'Gros Bleu' have a deep, almost navy blue color that dries well for potpourri. This variety has a light, clean lavender fragrance.

Lavandula ×intermedia 'Grosso'

Lavandula ×intermedia 'Hidcote Giant'

✳ 'Grosso'

ORIGIN: Pierre Grosso, Vaucluse District, France, about 1972
FLOWER COLOR: purple
FOLIAGE COLOR: gray-green
STEM LENGTH: 20–24 inches
BLOOMS: once in early summer
PLANT HEIGHT: 32–36 inches
SPACING: 36 inches
HARDINESS: zones 5–9

☙ The bloom habit of 'Grosso' creates an almost perfect 180-degree dome, like a hedgehog. The flower spikes are a bit darker than those of 'Fat Spike'. This variety has the highest oil content of all lavenders, and more than 70 percent of lavender oil produced in the world comes from 'Grosso'.

'Hidcote Giant'

ORIGIN: Major Lawrence Johnston, Hidcote Manor, Gloucester, England, before 1957
FLOWER COLOR: medium purple
FOLIAGE COLOR: gray-green
STEM LENGTH: 24–30 inches
BLOOMS: once in early summer
PLANT HEIGHT: 36–42 inches
SPACING: 42–48 inches
HARDINESS: zones 5–9

☙ The flower heads of 'Hidcote Giant' are amazingly large and plump. The flower fragrance is strong.

Lavandula ×intermedia 'Impress Purple'

Lavandula ×intermedia 'Provence'

'Impress Purple'

ORIGIN: France via New Zealand, 1983; named by Peter Smale, Redbank Research Centre, New Zealand, 1994
FLOWER COLOR: purple
FOLIAGE COLOR: gray-green
STEM LENGTH: 20–24 inches
BLOOMS: once in early summer
PLANT HEIGHT: 30–36 inches
SPACING: 36–42 inches
HARDINESS: zones 5–9

❧ 'Impress Purple' is a great choice for fresh bouquets. The dusty purple flower spikes appear brushed with silver when held up to the sun.

'Provence'

ORIGIN: Alpenglow Gardens, North Surrey, British Columbia, mid-1950s
FLOWER COLOR: light purple
FOLIAGE COLOR: green
STEM LENGTH: 24–30 inches
BLOOMS: once in early summer
PLANT HEIGHT: 48–60 inches
SPACING: 60–72 inches
HARDINESS: zones 5–9

❧ 'Provence' thrives in climates with dry summers. In wetter climates, this variety is prone to fungal diseases and can appear yellow after a period of time. The stems do not dry well for dried bouquets, as the lavender buds fall off easily.

Lavandula ×intermedia 'Silver Edge'

Lavandula ×intermedia 'Silver Leaf'

'Silver Edge'

ORIGIN: Walberton Nursery, West Sussex, England, around 1987
FLOWER COLOR: light purple
FOLIAGE COLOR: light green with creamy variegation on outside leaves
STEM LENGTH: 6–8 inches
BLOOMS: once in early summer
PLANT HEIGHT: 30–40 inches
SPACING: 42 inches
HARDINESS: zones 5–9

➤ This patented variety is one of the few variegated lavenders, making it a unique garden addition. The flowers are not as exceptional as the foliage.

'Silver Leaf'

ORIGIN: unknown
FLOWER COLOR: light purple
FOLIAGE COLOR: silver
STEM LENGTH: 18–20 inches
BLOOMS: once in early summer
PLANT HEIGHT: 36–42 inches
SPACING: 42–48 inches
HARDINESS: zones 5–9

➤ This is one of the last lavandins to bloom in late summer.

Lavandula ×intermedia 'Super'

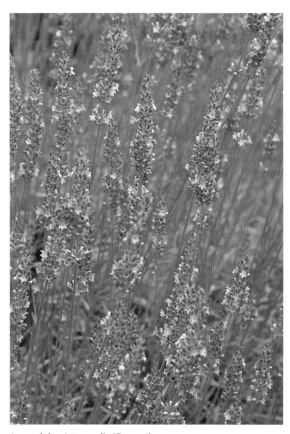

Lavandula ×intermedia 'Sussex'

'Super'

ORIGIN: Etablissements Chiris, Grasse, France, around 1956
FLOWER COLOR: light purple
FOLIAGE COLOR: gray-green
STEM LENGTH: 18–20 inches
BLOOMS: once in early summer
PLANT HEIGHT: 48–52 inches
SPACING: 60 inches
HARDINESS: zones 5–9

➥ 'Super' has a light, clean fragrance, similar to *Lavandula angustifolia*, and is often used for oil production.

'Sussex'

ORIGIN: Simon Charlesworth, Downderry Nursery, Kent, England, 1983
FLOWER COLOR: purple
FOLIAGE COLOR: gray-green
STEM LENGTH: 20–24 inches
BLOOMS: once in early summer
PLANT HEIGHT: 48–52 inches
SPACING: 60 inches
HARDINESS: zones 5–9

➥ This variety has been confused throughout the trade as 'Super' and 'Arabian Knight', but the blossoms are a bit darker than those of 'Super'.

Lavandula ×intermedia 'Tuscan Blue'

Lavandula ×intermedia 'Vera'

'Tuscan Blue'
also sold as 'Tuscan'

ORIGIN: unknown
FLOWER COLOR: medium blue
FOLIAGE COLOR: gray-green
STEM LENGTH: 18–20 inches
BLOOMS: once in early summer
PLANT HEIGHT: 36–40 inches
SPACING: 42–48 inches
HARDINESS: zones 5–9

☙ Not to be confused with the rosemary of the same name, 'Tuscan Blue' has a pleasing medium blue flower color.

'Vera'

ORIGIN: unknown
FLOWER COLOR: medium blue
FOLIAGE COLOR: green
STEM LENGTH: 18–20 inches
BLOOMS: once in early summer
PLANT HEIGHT: 36–48 inches
SPACING: 48 inches
HARDINESS: zones 5–9

☙ The 'Vera' described here is a *Lavandula ×intermedia* variety; however, 'Vera' is also offered as a variety of *L. angustifolia*.

Lavandula multifida

Lavandula multifida

Lavandula multifida is commonly referred to as fernleaf lavender and has also been called 'Pubescens' in the nursery trade. The fernlike foliage makes it an attractive plant for containers. However, this lavender's fragrance is less than appealing. Some claim it smells like burning rubber; I think it smells like skunk.

ORIGIN: native to Europe
FLOWER COLOR: dark blue
FOLIAGE COLOR: green
STEM LENGTH: 4–6 inches
BLOOMS: continuously starting in late spring
PLANT HEIGHT: 18–24 inches
SPACING: 24–30 inches
HARDINESS: zones 9–11

This tender lavender should be protected during the winter months. It generally lives only one or two years in containers but often reseeds itself and is easy to grow.

Lavandula stoechas

Lavandula stoechas is easily identified by its cylindrical flower heads wrapped with tiny flowers, topped with leaflike extensions called bracts that resemble rabbit ears or butterfly wings. The species name *stoechas* comes from *Stoechades*, the former name of the island group off the coast of France now known as Îles d'Hyères. *L. stoechas* is generally hardy from zone 7, but certain varieties tend to be tougher than others. Interestingly, darker cultivars seem to withstand colder temperatures than lighter-flowering lavenders. Pink-flowering stoechas varieties are particularly tender and should be covered or brought indoors during colder winter months.

Among the earliest lavenders to bloom, *Lavandula stoechas* will produce flowers all spring and summer. Pruning this species requires a different technique. The continual flowering means you will have to prune more often throughout the summer. Take the plant down by half after the first flush and continue to shape the foliage into a moundlike ball. The foliage tends to want to shoot up instead of out, so trim these shoots back to 3 or 4 inches above the hard wood. Some *L. stoechas* varieties, such as 'Van Gogh', have more of a spreading habit, so you will need to trim along the bottom of the plant as well. *L. stoechas* will reseed itself, so you may find tiny lavender plants growing around the base plant.

Stoechas varieties are a great choice for areas that have higher levels of humidity. They are not prone to sudden wilt, as some *Lavandula angustifolia* varieties are, and will thrive in high temperatures.

A few of the varieties listed here are actually hybrids with *Lavandula viridis* even though they are often grouped with stoechas lavenders. These hybrids carry some of the same characteristics as *L. viridis*, including similar fragrance (pungent, camphorous) and lighter foliage.

Lavandula stoechas in a mixed border

Lavandula 'Ballerina'

Lavandula stoechas 'Big Butterfly'

'Ballerina'

ORIGIN: Peter Carter, The Ploughman's Garden and Nursery, Waiuku, South Auckland, New Zealand, 1997
FLOWER COLOR: bicolor
FOLIAGE COLOR: light green
STEM LENGTH: 4–6 inches
BLOOMS: continuously starting in early spring
PLANT HEIGHT: 30–36 inches
SPACING: 36 inches
HARDINESS: Zones 7–10

•❧ 'Ballerina' is a hybrid with *Lavandula viridis*. Dark purple flower heads with creamy white bracts appear brushed with pink when the flowers have been open for a while. The top bracts resemble a ballerina's arms stretched in an arch above her head.

'Big Butterfly'

ORIGIN: unknown
FLOWER COLOR: plum
FOLIAGE COLOR: light green
STEM LENGTH: 6–8 inches
BLOOMS: continuously starting in spring
PLANT HEIGHT: 24–30 inches
SPACING: 30 inches
HARDINESS: zones 7–10

•❧ 'Big Butterfly' is distinctly different from *Lavandula stoechas* 'Butterfly', also known as 'James Compton'.

Lavandula 'Blue Star'

Lavandula stoechas 'Cottage Rose'

'Blue Star'

ORIGIN: Germany, 1990
FLOWER COLOR: plum
FOLIAGE COLOR: moss green
STEM LENGTH: 6–8 inches
BLOOMS: continuously starting in spring
PLANT HEIGHT: 20–24 inches
SPACING: 24–30 inches
HARDINESS: zones 7–10

➥ 'Blue Star' is a hybrid with *Lavandula viridis*. It looks like a smaller version of 'Helmsdale', with smaller flower heads and bracts.

'Cottage Rose'

ORIGIN: Van Hevelingen Herb Nursery, Newburg, Oregon, 2010
FLOWER COLOR: bicolor
FOLIAGE COLOR: green
STEM LENGTH: 4–6 inches
BLOOMS: continuously starting in early spring
PLANT HEIGHT: 20–24 inches
SPACING: 24–30 inches
HARDINESS: zones 8–10

➥ 'Cottage Rose' has dark fuchsia blossoms with beautiful light pink miniature top bracts. It would add a lovely color variation in the garden. 'Cottage Rose' is a selection from hardier seedlings of 'Barcelona Rose'.

Lavandula 'Helmsdale'

Lavandula stoechas 'Ivory Crown'

'Helmsdale'

ORIGIN: Geoff and Adair Genge, Marshwood
   Gardens, Invercargill, New Zealand, 1991
FLOWER COLOR: plum
FOLIAGE COLOR: moss green
STEM LENGTH: 2–4 inches
BLOOMS: continuously starting in spring
PLANT HEIGHT: 36–42 inches
SPACING: 42 inches
HARDINESS: zones 7–10

➥ 'Helmsdale' is a hybrid with *Lavandula viridis*.
It is one of the darkest-flowering *Lavandula stoechas*
cultivars available, making it a fantastic hedging
plant.

'Ivory Crown'

ORIGIN: Van Hevelingen Herb Nursery,
   Newburg, Oregon, year unknown
FLOWER COLOR: bicolor
FOLIAGE COLOR: light green
STEM LENGTH: 4–6 inches
BLOOMS: continuously starting in spring
PLANT HEIGHT: 20–24 inches
SPACING: 24–30 inches
HARDINESS: zones 7–10

➥ Deep blue spikes are topped with ivory bracts.

Lavandula stoechas 'James Compton'

Lavandula stoechas 'Madrid Blue'

'James Compton'
also sold as 'Butterfly'

ORIGIN: Jamie Compton, Chelsea Physic Garden, London, England, about 1979
FLOWER COLOR: plum
FOLIAGE COLOR: moss green
STEM LENGTH: 6–8 inches
BLOOMS: continuously starting in early spring
PLANT HEIGHT: 20–30 inches
SPACING: 30 inches
HARDINESS: zones 7–10

●❖ 'James Compton' has long flower stems, which is generally unusual in this lavender species, with extended top bracts in plum. Very unique.

'Madrid Blue'
also sold as 'Bee Happy'

ORIGIN: Bob Cherry and John Robb, Paradise Plants, Kulnura, New South Wales, Australia, 1997
FLOWER COLOR: bicolor
FOLIAGE COLOR: light green
STEM LENGTH: 6–8 inches
BLOOMS: continuously starting in spring
PLANT HEIGHT: 24–30 inches
SPACING: 30–36 inches
HARDINESS: zones 7–10

●❖ Light sky blue compact flower spikes are topped with creamy white bracts. Propagation for commercial purposes is prohibited as the Madrid Series is patented.

Lavandula stoechas 'Madrid Purple'

Lavandula stoechas 'Otto Quast'

'Madrid Purple'

ORIGIN: Bob Cherry and John Robb, Paradise Plants, Kulnura, New South Wales, Australia, 2001

FLOWER COLOR: plum

FOLIAGE COLOR: green

STEM LENGTH: 6–8 inches

BLOOMS: continuously starting in early spring

PLANT HEIGHT: 24–30 inches

SPACING: 30–36 inches

HARDINESS: zones 7–10

Another selection in the Madrid series, a collection of smaller, well-formed lavenders with blooms that last throughout the season.

'Otto Quast'

ORIGIN: Homestead Gardens, Santa Rosa, California, 1980

FLOWER COLOR: plum

FOLIAGE COLOR: moss green

STEM LENGTH: 2–4 inches

BLOOMS: continuously starting in early spring

PLANT HEIGHT: 25–30 inches

SPACING: 30 inches

HARDINESS: zones 7–10

This cultivar is generally available in most garden centers and is often grown from seed, making the true strain unreliable. It has a long-lasting dark plum flower head with slightly lighter-colored top bracts.

Lavandula stoechas 'Portuguese Giant'

Lavandula stoechas 'Red Star'

'Portuguese Giant'

ORIGIN: Van Hevelingen Herb Nursery, Newberg, Oregon, 2002
FLOWER COLOR: plum
FOLIAGE COLOR: green
STEM LENGTH: 10–12 inches
BLOOMS: continuously starting in spring
PLANT HEIGHT: 25–30 inches
SPACING: 30–36 inches
HARDINESS: zones 7–10

The flower heads of 'Portuguese Giant' are strikingly large and unusual, making it a great focal point in the garden.

'Red Star'

ORIGIN: Germany, 1990s
FLOWER COLOR: bicolor
FOLIAGE COLOR: moss green
STEM LENGTH: 4–6 inches
BLOOMS: continuously starting in early spring
PLANT HEIGHT: 24–30 inches
SPACING: 30–36 inches
HARDINESS: zones 7–10

'Red Star' has vivid compact fuchsia flower heads topped with light pink bracts.

Lavandula 'Regal Splendor'

Lavandula stoechas 'Sancho Panza'

'Regal Splendor'

ORIGIN: Marilyn and Ian Wightman, New Zealand, 1994
FLOWER COLOR: plum
FOLIAGE COLOR: green
STEM LENGTH: 2–4 inches
BLOOMS: continuously starting in early spring
PLANT HEIGHT: 25–30 inches
SPACING: 30–36 inches
HARDINESS: zones 7–10

🌿 'Regal Splendor' is a hybrid with *Lavandula viridis*. This showy, dark-flowering variety requires hard pruning to keep its shape.

'Sancho Panza'

ORIGIN: unknown
FLOWER COLOR: plum
FOLIAGE COLOR: light green
STEM LENGTH: 4–6 inches
BLOOMS: continuously starting in early spring
PLANT HEIGHT: 24–30 inches
SPACING: 30 inches
HARDINESS: zones 7–10

🌿 'Sancho Panza' has dense, blunt dark purple flower heads with slightly lighter purple top bracts.

Lavandula stoechas 'Spanish Curly Top'

Lavandula stoechas 'Sugarberry Ruffles'

'Spanish Curly Top'

ORIGIN: Rhonda Whetham, Forever Lavender, New Zealand, year unknown
FLOWER COLOR: plum
FOLIAGE COLOR: moss green
BLOOMS: continuously starting in early spring
STEM LENGTH: 8–10 inches
PLANT HEIGHT: 30–36 inches
SPACING: 36 inches
HARDINESS: zones 7–10

🪶 Though many *Lavandula stoechas* varieties have curly top bracts, the bracts of this deep plum-colored variety are noticeably curly.

'Sugarberry Ruffles'

ORIGIN: Plant Growers Australia Pty. Ltd., Wonga Park, Victoria, Australia, year unknown
FLOWER COLOR: plum
FOLIAGE COLOR: moss green
STEM LENGTH: 2–4 inches
BLOOMS: continuously starting in early spring
PLANT HEIGHT: 18–24 inches
SPACING: 24–30 inches
HARDINESS: zones 7–10

🪶 'Sugarberry Ruffles' is known to bloom a few weeks earlier than other stoechas lavenders. Propagation for commercial purposes is prohibited as this variety is patented.

Lavandula 'Van Gogh'

Lavandula 'Willow Vale'

'Van Gogh'

ORIGIN: bred in New Zealand, grower unknown, 1996
FLOWER COLOR: bicolor
FOLIAGE COLOR: green
STEM LENGTH: 4–6 inches
BLOOMS: continuously starting in spring
PLANT HEIGHT: 24–30 inches
SPACING: 30–36 inches
HARDINESS: zones 7–10

➦ 'Van Gogh' is a hybrid with *Lavandula viridis*. The flower heads are soft violet with bracts of creamy white. 'Van Gogh' likes to creep, so keep this in mind when pruning.

'Willow Vale'

ORIGIN: unknown breeder, New South Wales, 1992
FLOWER COLOR: bicolor
FOLIAGE COLOR: light green
STEM LENGTH: 4–6 inches
BLOOMS: continuously starting in early spring
PLANT HEIGHT: 15–18 inches
SPACING: 24 inches
HARDINESS: zones 7–10

➦ 'Willow Vale' is a hybrid with *Lavandula viridis*. Mature blossoms of this variety have delicate reddish purple top bracts.

Lavandula 'Wings of Night'

Lavandula stoechas 'Winter Bee'

'Wings of Night'

ORIGIN: unknown
FLOWER COLOR: plum
FOLIAGE COLOR: green
STEM LENGTH: 4–6 inches
BLOOMS: continuously starting in spring
PLANT HEIGHT: 18–24 inches
SPACING: 24–30 inches
HARDINESS: zones 7–10

●❖ 'Wings of Night' is a hybrid with *Lavandula viridis*. This is a pretty lavender with dark purple flower heads and plum-colored bracts, similar to 'Otto Quast'.

'Winter Bee'

ORIGIN: Larkman Nurseries Pty. Ltd., Lilydale, Victoria, Australia, 2001
FLOWER COLOR: purple
FOLIAGE COLOR: moss green
STEM LENGTH: 4–6 inches
BLOOMS: continuously starting in early spring
PLANT HEIGHT: 12–20 inches
SPACING: 24–30 inches
HARDINESS: zones 7–10

●❖ 'Winter Bee' is one of the earliest blooming lavenders in the spring. Propagation for commercial purposes is prohibited as this variety is patented.

Lavandula viridis

Lavandula viridis

Lavandula viridis is easily identified by its green flower heads with white flowers ringed in yellow and whitish-green bracts. It may be indigenous to southern climates, but it can withstand temperatures below freezing for short periods of time. Some believe this unusual lavender smells like lemons; it has a high camphor content, which may explain the lemony undertones.

ORIGIN: native to southwest Spain and southern Portugal
FLOWER COLOR: bicolor
FOLIAGE COLOR: chartreuse green
BLOOMS: continuously starting in spring
STEM LENGTH: 6–8 inches
PLANT HEIGHT: 36–42 inches
SPACING: 42 inches
HARDINESS: zones 7–10

The light yellow flower heads of this species turn brown quickly. Because of its color, it makes a good accent plant next to the lavandins.

Care and Cultivation:

From Planting to Pruning, Harvesting, and Drying

Lavender field, Purple Haze, Sequim, Washington

As gardeners, we take on the responsibility of nurturing and ultimately benefiting from the plants we grow. No matter what our expectations may be, these mysterious creatures may surprise us. We may practice all the tips and tricks we read about in books or hear from our fellow gardeners, but these little lives can have a plan of their own, much to our dismay or delight. It's no wonder the places that grow and sell plants are called nurseries. As with raising children, we need to meet certain care requirements to grow happy, healthy plants.

Soil Preparation

Lavender needs an area with adequate drainage. Lavenders are native to southern Europe, where poor, rocky soils are the norm. The Mediterranean region boasts well-drained alkaline soils with lots of sunshine. Even though your garden may not have these same characteristics, having the right information to determine your soil texture and structure will allow you to work with the soil you have and amend it properly.

We often hear terms to describe soil such as sandy loam, clay, and silt, but what do they really mean? Soil texture is determined by the mineral content of your soil or the size of these particles in relation to one another. Larger particles create more air spaces, known as pores, which create better drainage. Pores allow for water and air to move through the soil. Rocky soils with more sand have the best drainage. Clay soils have smaller particles that make the soil hard and hold in more moisture. Silt falls somewhere in between the two. A good balance among sand, clay, and silt results in a substance called loam that is high in nutrients, well draining, and great for plants. The ideal soil texture for growing lavender is a sandy loam with larger particles for air and water to move through.

Soil structure describes how soil particles clump together to create your growing environment. Clumps of soil that form contain a variety of particles, big and small, that allow for movement in the soil. These clumps are called aggregates and make up the soil space for water, air, and roots to move through. Air is an important factor in soil structure as it creates room for water to drain. Lavender needs a loose soil structure to allow it to grow properly. If your soil structure allows for adequate drainage, you do not need to amend the soil. But if your soil is more clay than anything else and drains poorly, there are things you can do to improve soil texture and structure. Don't let clay soil stop you from growing lavender.

One option to deal with clay soil is to mound your lavender plants. Create a planting mound above your existing soil that measures at least a foot high and a foot wide. If you are planting a row of lavender, create a mound a foot high and a foot wide as long as you would like your row to be. Even out your mound on top, making sure it doesn't form a pyramidal shape, as this could expose the roots and cause the plant to die. Mounding like this can improve soil structure by allowing for better air flow and reducing compaction.

Heavy, slow-draining soils can be amended with a liberal dose of organic matter. Mushroom compost helps with soil aeration. Composted leaves are also an excellent choice to mix into your soil. Perlite and pumice, minerals mined from volcanic rock, have been used to improve soil aeration, but they have their drawbacks. Pumice creates aeration in the soil yet can hold moisture for a short period of time; perlite is effective yet is extremely light and will float to the top of your soil, which can create a mess. I have often heard of people adding sand to clay to improve drainage, but in my experience this creates a cementlike texture that is not good for

The payoff from care and cultivation: lavender bunches for drying

lavender. The best option for clay soil is a lot of organic matter, a shovel or a tiller, and a strong back.

An old gardener's adage says it's better to dig a $100 hole for a $10 plant than a $10 hole for a $100 plant. How true this is when it comes to clay soil! Lavender roots eventually cover an area about a foot in diameter, so keep this in mind when digging your hole.

Mediterranean herbs like lavender can tolerate sandy soils. Sandy soils tend to be low in nutrients, and this might inhibit growth in other plants, but not in lavender. Once lavender is in the ground, it does not need a significant amount of nitrogen to thrive. In fact, too much nitrogen will inhibit flower production while creating bushy green foliage. If you have sandy soil, you may want to add some compost when planting initially, but after that a dose of fertilizer low in nitrogen or no fertilizer at all is best.

Even though lavender doesn't need regular fertilization to thrive, starting plants in a soil that is rich in nutrients will give them a proper foundation. If you don't know what type of soil you have, a soil test can help. Do-it-yourself kits available at garden centers can test the nutrient content of your soil, but you may not have to get that technical. Dig up some of your soil. Is it easy to work your shovel into or are you struggling to dig a hole? Do you see bugs and worms working their way through the dirt or is your soil barren of beneficial organisms? Answering questions like these will help you determine what to do.

Understanding pH Levels

We often hear about pH levels and how important it is to have the right pH level in your soil. What does this mean exactly, and what does pH have to do with growing lavender? Basically, soil pH measures how many hydrogen ions are affecting plant roots. The more hydrogen ions in the soil, the more acidic the soil will be. The pH scale represents a soil's alkalinity or acidity, with soils that are more acidic measuring 0 to 6 and soils that are more alkaline measuring 8 to 14 on the pH scale. A pH of 7 is considered neutral. Acid soils are often referred to as sour, and alkaline soils are considered sweet.

The pH Scale

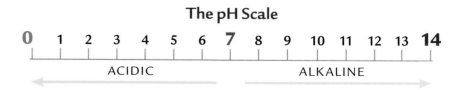

Many plants require specific pH levels to thrive. Plants like rhododendrons and blueberries like acidic soil. Lavender likes neutral soil and grows best with a pH of 6.5 to 7.5. When you grow lavender with other plants, it is best to choose those that have relatively the same pH requirements. The good news is that most ornamental plants like neutral soil.

How do you determine your pH levels? Tests are readily available at most garden centers. Areas that have heavy rainfall, such as the Pacific Northwest, tend to have more acidic soils. In drier parts of the country, soils tend to be more alkaline. If your soil is too acidic, you can add lime to raise the pH; dolomitic and calcitic lime are sold in powdered or pelletized form. Raising the pH in the soil is a slow process, and it can take a few months to register a change. Periodic tests will determine if your soil is at the correct level.

If your soil is too alkaline, adding sphagnum peat (which has a pH of 3.0 to 4.5) and organic matter will help lower your pH. Peat works well in smaller garden areas but may not be cost effective for larger areas. Granular sulfur is effective on a larger scale to lower pH but can take longer to work. It is important to follow the application instructions when using this product.

Fertilizer

Plants require several nutrients to thrive, but the three most common are nitrogen (N), phosphorus (P), and potassium (K). The numbers on most fertilizer containers tell us what percentage by volume of each nutrient the fertilizer contains. Many all-purpose nonorganic fertilizers are listed as 20-20-20; this means 20 percent N, 20 percent P, and 20 percent K, with other nutrients making up the rest of the mix. Organic fertilizers generally have lower numbers. Lavender does not need much fertilizer to thrive—at least, not in the traditional sense like other plants—but fertilizer can be beneficial if you are trying to add specific nutrients to achieve a particular objective.

The main function of nitrogen is to promote foliage growth. With smaller plants that are just starting out, nitrogen can help boost plant establishment, but too much nitrogen can put a great deal of energy into leaf production at the expense of flower yield. In fact, too much nitrogen will diminish flower production significantly. For this reason, it is best to avoid fertilizers high in nitrogen such as blood meal or liquid fish emulsion unless you are growing plants from starts. Once your lavender is established, you may choose to use a low-nitrogen fertilizer to establish stronger roots and help with the overall health of your plant.

Phosphorus is an important nutrient required for root development and overall plant health. It can be beneficial to add phosphorus right before lavender begins to bloom to give it an extra boost. Natural sources of phosphorous include bone meal and bat guano.

Potassium, also called potash, is a key nutrient to boost plants' tolerance to stresses such as varying temperatures or long periods of drought. Some growers believe it is a good idea to give lavender a dose of fertilizer with higher percentages of potassium to strengthen the plant through the winter. Lavender will then store the nutrients it needs during dormancy. Natural sources include composted fruits and vegetables and kelp meal.

Growing Lavender from Seeds

Lavender can be propagated in a couple of ways: from seeds and from cuttings. The former is known as sexual reproduction and the latter as asexual reproduction. Lavender seeds will not grow true to variety, so your new plants will be variations of the parent plant, whereas plants from cuttings are the same as the parent plant. You can try propagating plants by both methods.

The process by which a seed is produced begins when plant sperm or pollen is deposited by means of wind, insects, or humans into the ovary of

Fresh lavender with chaff (seed husks) and seeds

another plant in the same species but not necessarily of the same variety. When an insect visits a flower, the pollen, located in the stamen, attaches to the insect and is deposited into the ovary of the next flower, where it joins with an ovule or egg. After fertilization, the ovule develops into a seed. Unless this process is closely monitored and insects are not allowed to cross-pollinate, the seed can have parents that are genetically different and thus will not grow into a recognizable cultivar.

Once lavender flowers open and dry, they drop tiny seeds that are suitable for planting. The shelf life of lavender seeds is only about a year, so it is best to plant them as soon as you can. Store seeds in the refrigerator to prolong planting. Those seeds that do sprout can take up to three months to grow roots enough to transplant in the garden or a container. Once they bloom, they will most likely not look like the plant in the picture on your seed packet as little care has been taken over the years to prevent hybridized seeds. Lavender seed labeled 'Hidcote' or 'Munstead' is really just seed-grown *Lavandula angustifolia* and cannot be considered true to name. If you like the cottage look and don't mind lavender plants with variation, this may be a good choice for you. However, if you want your plant to match the description, it's best to buy lavender that has been grown from cuttings. That said, digging up new seedlings can yield beautiful surprises that could grow into great lavenders. Many new varieties have come into the trade this way.

Most of the time, two different species of lavender that have been crossed do not produce viable seed and are sterile. *Lavandula ×intermedia* varieties like 'Grosso' and 'Provence' can only be reproduced using vegetative methods. Mother Nature can throw in some surprises, however, and a few hybrid varieties have been known to throw fertile seed.

Growing Lavender from Cuttings

Asexual reproduction or plant cloning involves taking a cutting or graft from an existing mother plant and rooting it to make a new plant. This process ensures the new plant will be the same as the plant the cutting was taken from. Growing lavender from cuttings is a fairly easy procedure you can do yourself.

Lavender starts can be grown from softwood or hardwood cuttings. Softwood is new growth that is still pliable; hardwood is mature stems that will snap if bent. Softwood cuttings should be taken in spring during active growth, but hardwood cuttings can be taken in either spring or fall. Which type of cutting you choose to grow depends on the plant. Lavender plants that are continuous bloomers, such as *Lavandula angustifolia* 'Buena

Vista', are more difficult to root because they want to bloom throughout the rooting process, so propagation from hardwood cuttings is recommended. *Lavandula stoechas* varieties fall into this category as well.

Softwood cuttings are more plentiful, but hardwood cuttings can yield a higher rate of germination. Hardwood usually takes a bit longer to grow a root, but the success rate can be slightly higher. *Lavandula angustifolia* varieties take longer to root and are slower to grow into larger plants. *Lavandula ×intermedia* varieties tend to root faster under the right conditions, generally within two to three weeks.

Cuttings taken in the fall should be collected before the first frost so as not to damage the plant while it goes into dormancy. Many growers choose to take cuttings in the fall because this timing allows the starts to go through a process known as vernalization, also called hardening off. In this process, a plant is exposed to cold for a period of time to strengthen it and increase flower production. When a rooted cutting is allowed to go dormant, generally for six weeks or more, the plant goes through its natural cycle, allowing it to come out of dormancy tougher and more stable. If you don't have a greenhouse, bringing your new plants outdoors for short periods of time during the day, then bringing them inside at night will gradually get them used to the elements. Eventually, you can leave them outside for longer periods of time. Just make sure the temperature variation is not too extreme as this can stress your plants. If you take a cutting

The two kinds of cuttings: hardwood (top) and softwood (bottom)

Rooting a Lavender Cutting

If you talk to ten different plant growers, you will probably get ten different methods for plant propagation. You can get poor results from one method, then change one step and have wonderful success. The steps here have worked well for me, but some experimentation may be in order, depending on your environment and access to materials.

What you will need:

◈ **sharp knife or razor blade**

◈ **rooting hormone, liquid or powder form**

◈ **rooting soil—a mix of 60 percent perlite or vermiculite, 30 percent peat moss, and 10 percent bark—or propagation soil available at most garden centers**

◈ **clean, sterilized container to hold the soil with holes for drainage**

1. To take a hardwood cutting, find a branch close to the base of the plant and feel for a bump, indicating a leaf node. Using sharp, clean pruning shears or scissors, cut a 3- to 4-inch piece at a 45-degree angle just below the node. For a softwood cutting, clip a 3- to 4-inch continuous piece from the tip of a growing stem.

2. Pull off the leaves from the bottom 2 inches of the cutting.

3. Using a sharp, clean knife, scrape the skin off the bottom portion of the cutting on one side.

4. Put the rooting soil in the container and water it well. Dip the cutting in the rooting hormone and stick it into the soil.

5. Keep the soil moist and the cutting warm through the rooting process, which may take up to four weeks. A consistent temperature of 68 to 70 degrees is optimal for getting the plants to root. Heat mats are a good option. You may also cover the cutting with a plastic bag or container to keep heat in and maintain humidity, but this method requires careful monitoring to make sure the plant does not become too hot. Placing unrooted cuttings under florescent heat lamps in your home in a protected area will yield positive results as well.

6. Check for roots after a few weeks by *gently* tugging on the cutting.

7. Transplant your rooted cutting into a larger container. Water it in and then allow it to go a bit on the dry side. Water occasionally but do not allow it to get too wet. Lavender does not like wet feet for too long. Feed with an all-purpose fertilizer to promote growth. Make sure your new start is protected from extreme elements such as high heat or frost.

8. When your lavender begins to grow, it will produce a top shoot that will need to be snipped off level with the rest of the foliage to force it to branch. You may have to trim the foliage a few times to train your plant to grow the way you want it to. If you want a topknot effect, do not trim the top but allow it to grow straight up. Remove foliage from the bottom of your start. Eventually your plant will accumulate foliage at the top.

in the fall for spring planting, the entire process will take about eight months from cutting to 4-inch plant. Your lavender should then be ready for spring planting.

Irrigation

Lavender can tolerate wet weather while it is dormant if the soil drains well. But once the weather changes and lavender is exposed to warmer temperatures, it does not like wet foliage for long periods of time. Overhead watering can contribute to fungal diseases, and it can also split the plant and cause it to become woody. When you water your lavender, it is best to use a drip system or water at the base with a wand.

Even though lavender is drought tolerant, it needs some water to become established once planted. Giving your lavender a good soak and then allowing it to go slightly dry before watering again for the first few months after planting will help the plant root and become acclimated to your environment. Once your lavender becomes established, it may not need supplemental water in the summer months. In areas that receive high rainfall during winter and spring, plants generally get enough hydration to last through the summer months.

If you live in an excessively hot area, knowing when to water your lavender can be tricky. Extended watering during spring and summer months

Watering lavender with drip irrigation

can cause root rot and be detrimental to your plant. Not enough water in hot weather over long stretches may stress your lavender. If you live in an area with little rainfall, water your lavender once every few weeks during the hottest summer months.

What's Wrong with My Lavender?

Like many organisms in nature, plants live by the code "survival of the fittest." Healthy, well-cared-for plants tend to stay that way because they do not have weaknesses for pests and diseases to exploit. When a plant is stressed, nature has a way of getting rid of it. Air- or soil-borne pathogens can cause it to turn brown, wilt, or show black mold. Sometimes pests will attack the weak parts of the plant, making the leaves curl and wilt. Purchasing healthy, disease-free plant material from a reputable nursery is your first step to success. The rest involves due diligence and following a few simple guidelines.

Determining just exactly what is causing lavender to appear unhealthy can be a tricky process. Most problems can be eliminated by evaluating a few factors. Poor drainage is the number one cause of plant loss. If water is allowed to pool at the base of a lavender plant, it will eventually succumb to root rot and part, if not all, of the plant will die. Soil with good aeration is paramount to keeping a lavender plant healthy.

Winter dieback

Yellowing lavender can mean different things. When leaves on a container plant turn yellow, it normally is an indication that the plant is either lacking in or getting too much nitrogen. Lavender in the ground is different. Yellow leaves can mean the plant is getting too much water and drainage needs to be addressed. Mulching with gravel or sand can decrease water concentration around the base of the plant. Yellow leaves can also result from harvesting the flowers too late in the season. When flowers are left too long on the lavender plant, it can stress the foliage. This issue usually resolves itself once new growth appears on the foliage after the flowers are harvested. Lavender plants can also turn yellow due to a fungal problem, especially when the yellow is accompanied with a smoky gray or black tint.

Fungus spores are tiny pathogens that can live almost anywhere. They can spread around your yard and cause plant stress or death. Two of the most common fungal diseases are phytophthora root rot and botrytis or gray mold. They appear when moisture is allowed to sit on the foliage for too long or when the plant is not allowed to breathe because it is too crowded by other plants and airflow is obstructed. Luckily there are things you can do to reduce or alleviate air- and soil-borne diseases in your yard.

◈ **Use clean tools.** After a long day in the garden, it may be difficult to remember to clean your garden tools, but this step is necessary, especially since you use these tools from plant to plant, making it easier to spread diseases. Having a spray bottle filled with bleach or alcohol and water on hand and spraying down your tools before you put them away is a good practice. Spray work surfaces down as well. Wash garden gloves or use disposable ones.

◈ **Remove plant debris.** Fungus loves dead or dying plant material and will live there until it gets a chance to infect your plants. Lavender needs good airflow, not only between plants but also at the base of the plant. Excessive leaves and soil that build up at the base of the plant may eventually contribute to root rot. Mulching with matter such as sand, gravel, or well-draining compost can give your plant added benefits. If you put your leaves in a compost pile, make sure plant matter is composted thoroughly.

◈ **Trim your plants.** Lavender likes to be trimmed. In fact, giving your lavender a good haircut in the spring not only promotes healthy new growth but can also reduce the possibility of fungal diseases.

◈ **Leave room between plants.** We all like the look of lavender growing together in one long row, but in areas of high rainfall or humidity, this can be detrimental to your lavender plants. Make sure you follow spacing recommendations and allow adequate room between plants. This will not only help alleviate fungal disease, it will also increase flower production by allowing room for the plant to bloom in a uniform circle.

Pesky Bugs and Critters

Lavender can be bothered by a few pesky bugs and critters. Foremost among these are spittle bugs, aphids, grasshoppers, and moles and voles. Check your plants regularly for any sign of these so that you can catch any problem early and deal with it accordingly.

Spittle bugs, also known as frog hoppers, generally come out in early spring after lying dormant on plant material throughout the winter. These tiny, fluorescent green creatures secrete a spitlike froth, then cover themselves in what looks like saliva. This odd process protects them from predators and makes them virtually impossible to see, unless you unearth them from their bubbly cocoons. Spittle bugs really like lavender plants and may produce several globs on one plant. Although they feed on plant sap, they really do not do much damage. If they are too unsightly for you, a good

Left: The "spit" produced by a spittle bug
Right: The critter itself

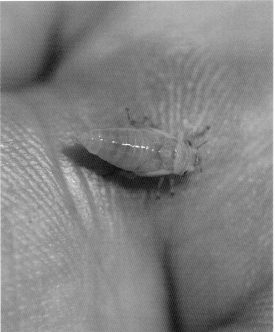

spray with the hose will generally get rid of them; no pesticide is needed. Their stay is short, and they are gone once the weather warms up a bit.

You may know about aphids on roses, but aphids can appear on certain varieties of lavender as well, namely *Lavandula stoechas* or *L. viridis* species. These tiny green or black insects feed on new plant growth while emitting a sticky substance that causes the leaves to twist and weaken. A spray solution of liquid dish soap and water will usually kill them right away. Make sure to look for new eggs after they appear and reapply as needed. Ladybugs love to eat aphids, so releasing them in your garden can be a benefit as well.

A lavender grower in Idaho had a horrible infestation of grasshoppers that ate her lavender one season. This area had particular trouble with grasshoppers eating various crops, and apparently they liked the taste of lavender as well. If grasshoppers become a problem for you, grasshopper bait, sold under a variety of brand names, may be a solution. If you have chickens, they love to eat grasshoppers, so let them loose in your garden.

Moles, voles, and other furry creatures can be the bane of your gardening existence. They dig tunnels below ground; moles look for insects and worms, while voles feast on the tender roots of your lavender. They like to follow a water line, so drip irrigation can give them incentive to follow a row of lavender. When lavender plants look dead on one side, this may be

Mole damage along a line of lavender

the reason. How humane or inhumane you choose to be in dealing with these critters is up to you. There are a wide range of deterrents and traps on the market to deal with them.

Pruning Your Lavender Plant

The number one reason a lavender plant looks shabby is that it has received improper pruning from the very beginning. If you follow these simple steps, you will have a mounded, well-shaped, healthy lavender plant that will last for many years to come. Remember, lavender likes to be pruned, so don't be afraid to take it back a bit to prevent your plant from getting too woody.

The first prune. We all love to buy that perfect lavender plant at the nursery or garden center. The blooms are beautiful, and we can't wait to put it into the ground to enhance our existing garden. After a period of time, the flowers start to die back and we may forget to trim it before fall arrives. What happens? Working to produce those beautiful flowers has taken the energy that otherwise would have been used to form the foliage. After a period of time, if the flowers have not been removed, the plant will show signs of stress and will compensate by branching out in different

From left to right: first-, second-, and third-year lavender plants

Top left: A lavender plant after the first flush and before pruning

Top right: Removing new growth to strengthen foliage and encourage flowering

directions. By next spring, when the plant produces more flowers, the significant energy loss the plant has suffered due to improper pruning will cause the base of the plant to become woody.

Even though we want that instant gratification in our gardens, it is best to show restraint by sacrificing for the greater good. What this means is that you should prune the flowers off your lavender plant when you put it into the ground. This may be difficult, but the results in the long run will far outweigh the aggravation; otherwise, in a few years you will be pulling out that shabby lavender plant. The plant you put into the ground should be well shaped to begin with. If not, you may want to trim around the plant a bit in the beginning to encourage new growth. Your plant may bloom again during the season, depending on the type of lavender, and these blooms should be removed at the end of the summer. Lavender grows fast, so if you plant in the spring, it could double in size by fall.

Year two. When your lavender plant comes out of dormancy and starts to grow foliage, this is the time to prune in year two. Using sharp, clean shears, remove the new growth all over the plant. This will invigorate your plant and encourage more flowers to form.

When your plant produces flowers in the second year, enjoy the bounty

A lavender plant
after pruning

A lavender plant that has
become woody

but do harvest them before fall. If your plant is an early or continuous bloomer, harvesting the flowers after the first flush will allow for consecutive flowering in the same season. By this point, your lavender plant will begin to take on a moundlike appearance. Pruning the plant into a ball will keep the foliage tight and compact while training the plant to take this shape.

Year three. By the third year, your lavender plant will be considered full grown, but it will continue to grow larger until year five. If you have pruned it properly in the first two years, your plant will have a nice rounded shape that will produce a full harvest, depending on the variety. When lavender is fully formed, it usually does not require hard pruning. We give our lavender a slight trim after harvest, but spring pruning once the plant is established is not necessary. If a lavender is a continuous or double bloomer, the stems and flowers should be removed before the winter months. Pruning your lavender plants using this method will not only improve the health of your plant but also allow you to enjoy it for many years to come.

Once a plant has become woody and sprawly, it is nearly impossible to retrain it with pruning. Cutting into the hard wood is detrimental to the plant and can cause it to die. It is best to remove it and start from scratch.

Harvesting Lavender

A first-year lavender plant will produce only a few stems, and it is best to trim these before they flower completely to strengthen the plant. By year two, your lavender will normally double in size and will produce two or three small bunches, depending on the type of lavender. From year two to year three, your plant will grow quite a bit bigger, normally by two-thirds, so you will have an abundance of flowers in the third year.

The ideal tool for harvesting lavender consists of a curved, serrated blade with a handle. Lavender is tough, so don't be afraid to grab a bunch and cut a handful. Harvesting tools are available online or at garden shows.

Lavender blooms at different times throughout the season. How fast your lavender flowers is dependent on the weather. Early bloomers usually

Harvesting lavender with a curved, serrated blade

flower in May where I live in the Northwest, while others don't bloom until August here. When you harvest really depends on what you are going to do with your lavender after it is cut. If you don't plan to create something with it, be it a fresh bunch or a wreath, leave the flowers on the plant to enjoy. Just make sure you cut the stems back after the bloom cycle is finished. Waiting too long to harvest the flowers can stress your plant. Lavender varieties that bloom more than once in a season should be trimmed back anyway to allow for additional flowerings.

If you plan to use your lavender in crafts or cooking, keep your eye on the lavender buds and harvest the entire plant once a few flowers have

Top and bottom:
A harvested bunch

begun to emerge from the lavender buds. This technique minimizes shedding and keeps the lavender buds tight on the stem for later use. When a lavender bunch sheds, it is because too many flowers were allowed to open before harvesting.

Drying Lavender for Later Use

Once lavender has been harvested, you can put a fresh bunch in a vase or dry it for later use. Lavender placed in water will get moldy fairly quickly, so change the water frequently. Once lavender is placed in water, you shouldn't take it out and try to dry it. Lavender stems that have been soaked in water will not dry well.

To dry lavender, cut a bunch with approximately a hundred stems and bundle with a rubber band toward the bottom of the bunch. Pull apart a paper clip and thread one end through the rubber band. Hang your bunch from a chain or rope, upside down in a warm, dark, dry room with adequate circulation. Your bunch should be dry within a few weeks. This method preserves the color of the flower buds and keeps the lavender from getting moldy.

Dried lavender bunches will keep for many years but may lose their fragrance after a season. To release the lavender scent, give your dried bunch a squeeze. Lavender with a higher oil content, such as *Lavandula ×intermedia* 'Grosso', will stay fragrant longer.

Drying lavender bunches
upside down in a warm,
dry room

Lavender Recipes:

Herb Blends, Condiments, Desserts, and Drinks

Luscious bunches at
Barn Owl Nursery,
Wilsonville, Oregon

Using lavender as an herb to enhance the flavor of food and drink has increased in popularity over the last few years. Many are surprised to find out that lavender adds a floral note that is distinctive and delicious. Lavender is an herb just like mint, thyme, and rosemary, but what differentiates lavender from other herbs is its versatility. This chapter offers recipes incorporating lavender in a variety of dishes and beverages.

Lavender adds sweetness to dessert recipes like cookies and ice cream, and is a subtle complement to savory dishes like meats and vegetables. Lavender is also wonderful in drinks. You will be hooked on lavender lemonade after the first sip. Warm teas made with lavender are not only tasty but also have health benefits. Mint tea has been known as a remedy for an upset stomach; since lavender is in the mint family, it has the same advantageous qualities. Its reputation for easing tension and insomnia and aiding digestion makes a cup of warm lavender tea a bedtime staple.

Choosing the Right Lavender for Your Recipe

The kind of lavender you choose to use in recipes depends on individual tastes. Every lavender variety has a particular phytochemistry that yields a distinctive flavor. *Lavandula ×intermedia* cultivars are generally higher in camphor, an organic chemical compound that can produce a bitter flavor. For this reason, most varieties of *L. ×intermedia* or lavandins are not a good choice for culinary use, with the exception of *L. ×intermedia* 'Provence', which is lower in camphor and milder than other varieties in the same species. *Lavandula angustifolia* varieties have a sweeter taste with very little camphor flavor, so these varieties are generally preferred in lavender dishes. *Lavandula stoechas* varieties are generally not used in cooking as these species tend to yield a bitter flavor. Which culinary lavender you use should be based on what tastes best to you, so try an assortment and decide for yourself. You can purchase culinary lavender or snip some from your garden.

As with any other herb, you can use fresh or dried lavender in your recipes. Keep in mind that drying lavender intensifies the flavor, so using a third of the amount of fresh lavender called for is recommended. To cull your own dried lavender for recipes, start with a fully dried bunch. Remove the buds from the stem by rolling it on a screen or rubbing it between your palms. Once the lavender buds are removed, place them in a colander and sift to remove debris. You can store dried lavender buds in an airtight container for several months.

These whole flower buds can be used in recipes but will release a strong dose of lavender flavor once consumed. One alternative is to use an herb grinder, food processor, or mortar and pestle to granulate dried lavender. This process will concentrate the lavender even more, so it is best to err on the conservative side when adding crushed lavender to dishes. Lavender is meant to enhance flavor, not overpower other ingredients.

Fresh lavender adds a light floral note to just about any dish. One technique involves steeping fresh lavender buds in liquid, then removing the lavender. Infusing lavender in this way creates a base that can be used in many drink, ice cream, and dessert recipes. Dried lavender can also be used as an infusion, as well as other dried herbs.

Lavender and sage in Dot Carson's raised herb garden, designed by Phil Thurnburg, Winterbloom

Best Lavenders for Culinary Use

These varieties have proved to taste the best in favorite recipes.

Lavandula angustifolia 'Buena Vista'

L. angustifolia 'Folgate'

L. angustifolia 'Hidcote Pink'

L. angustifolia 'Melissa'

L. angustifolia 'Royal Velvet'

Herb Blends with Lavender

Herbes de Provence is an enticing blend of Mediterranean herbs used as an all-purpose seasoning for various meat and vegetable dishes. The combinations of these herbs are numerous and can include up to eleven herbs in different amounts. Thyme is a constant. Other herbs usually included are rosemary, summer or winter savory, marjoram, and basil; mint, oregano, sage, and crushed bay leaf may also be included. In France, lavender is generally not used in herbes de Provence, but it has become a favorite ingredient in North America. Each ingredient contributes a unique touch of sweetness or pungency, depending on the herb. Experimentation is the best way to find a blend that works for you.

You can also use a blend of fresh herbs as a baster. Gather fresh herbs such as lavender, rosemary, and sage and bundle them with twine or a rubber band like a bouquet. Then use as a basting brush to add flavor to baked dishes. One more variation on the herb blend theme is bouquet garni. Wrap fresh or dried herbs in cheesecloth or bundle them with twine and simmer them in soups and sauces to flavor. Remove the herbs when the dish is complete.

Fresh and dried herbs
for culinary use

HERBES DE PROVENCE

This herbes de Provence recipe uses six different herbs, including lavender. You can use this blend in the Provençal Salmon and Pasta and the Mediterranean Chicken recipes that follow, or you can experiment to find a custom blend you like better. This recipe is adapted from one developed by Chris Mulder of Barn Owl Nursery.

> **1 tablespoon dried thyme leaves**
> **1 tablespoon dried basil leaves**
> **2 teaspoons dried culinary lavender buds**
> **2 teaspoons dried rosemary leaves**
> **½ teaspoon dried summer savory leaves**
> **½ teaspoon dried marjoram leaves**

♣ Mɪx all of the ingredients well and crush with a mortar and pestle or use an herb grinder. Store the mixture in an airtight glass or ceramic container for up to several months.

YOUR OWN CUSTOM HERB BLEND

    1½ teaspoons dried thyme
    1½ teaspoons dried marjoram
    1 teaspoon each of any or all of the following dried herbs:
        culinary lavender buds
        summer or winter savory leaves
        fennel seeds
        basil leaves
        mint leaves
        oregano leaves

❧ Mix all of the ingredients well and crush with a mortar and pestle or use an herb grinder. Store the mixture in an airtight glass or ceramic container for up to several months.

Tips to Find the Perfect Herb Blend for You

 Remember to write down each herb and the exact amount you use. Mix a small amount into cottage cheese, cream cheese, or butter. Place the herb cheese or butter in a small covered glass or ceramic dish in the refrigerator. Let it sit for a few hours or overnight before tasting. Spread the herb cheese or butter on plain crackers or bread to taste. Decide if you want to add more or less of one particular herb. Begin experimenting by adding a small amount of your blend to a range of foods. Try your blend in soups, stews, sauces, dressings, red meat marinades, and poultry dishes.

PROVENÇAL SALMON AND PASTA
Serves 2 to 4

This is an easy dish to prepare, with mouthwatering results. You can substitute tuna or another type of white fish for the salmon.

1 cup dried penne pasta
2 fresh salmon steaks cut approximately ¾ inch thick
1 teaspoon herbes de Provence
1 cup sliced fresh mushrooms
   (button, Portobello, or shitake mushrooms)
⅓ cup dry white wine
2 tablespoons prepared basil pesto
1 tablespoon lemon juice
2 teaspoons drained capers
1 tablespoon olive oil

1. Prepare penne pasta in advance by boiling in lightly salted water for 4 minutes. Drain pasta and set aside. Do not rinse.

2. Sprinkle salmon steaks on both sides with herbes de Provence. If desired, add a dash of salt.

3. In a medium bowl combine the partially cooked pasta, mushrooms, wine, pesto, lemon juice, and capers. Set aside.

4. Add olive oil to a large skillet and heat on medium-high. Brown the seasoned salmon steaks for one minute on each side. Reduce heat to medium.

5. Spoon the pasta mixture over and around the salmon in the skillet. Cover and let simmer for 9 minutes or until the salmon flakes easily with a fork.

MEDITERRANEAN CHICKEN
Serves 4 to 6

It doesn't take long to make this delicious and easy recipe. Provolone cheese is a good substitute for the feta.

> **2 teaspoons olive oil**
> **2 tablespoons white wine**
> **6 skinless, boneless chicken breasts, cubed**
> **3 cloves garlic, minced**
> **½ cup diced onion**
> **4 cups diced fresh tomatoes or 2 large cans (up to 32 ounces total) of diced tomatoes, drained**
> **½ cup white wine**
> **3 tablespoons herbes de Provence**
> **8 ounces pasta (rotini, farfalle, penne, or fusilli work well), cooked**
> **½ cup halved kalamata olives**
> **½ cup feta cheese**
> **¼ cup chopped fresh parsley (optional)**
> **salt and pepper to taste**

1. Heat the oil and 2 tablespoons white wine in a large skillet over medium heat. Add the cubed chicken and sauté for 5 minutes. Remove the chicken from the pan with a slotted spoon and set aside.

2. Sauté the garlic in the pan drippings for 30 seconds, then add the onion and sauté an additional 3 minutes. Add the tomatoes and bring to a boil. Reduce the heat, then add ½ cup of white wine and simmer for 10 minutes. Add the herbes de Provence and simmer for 5 more minutes. Meanwhile, prepare the pasta as directed and set aside.

3. Return the chicken to the skillet and cover. Simmer over low heat until the chicken is cooked thoroughly. Add the olives and the pasta to the mixture and simmer, stirring for 1 minute.

4. Sprinkle with the feta cheese and fresh parsley and serve.

Lavender Condiments

Lavender can be used to flavor a variety of condiments, from sugar and jam to vinegar and oil. These lavender-infused versions will add a tasty floral hint to recipes you might use them in.

LAVENDER SUGAR
Makes 2 cups

Sugar with culinary lavender buds

Lavender sugar can be used as a substitute for granulated sugar in all your favorite recipes. Adding lavender sugar to desserts and drinks will delight your family and friends and keep them coming back for more. Lavender sugar can be prepared either by infusing the flavor of lavender into the sugar and then removing it, or by mixing culinary lavender in with the sugar. Either method will work well. Keep in mind that lavender that has been crushed will be stronger, so use less than you would with whole buds. Leaving the lavender in the sugar will add a slight hint of color to your recipes and make for a nice presentation in a glass jar. The amount of lavender you choose to use depends on personal preference. The taste of lavender will begin to fade after 6 months or so.

1 tablespoon dried culinary lavender buds
1 cup granulated or powdered sugar

❖ In a spice grinder or food processor, pulse the lavender and sugar until finely ground. Transfer to an airtight container and store in a dry area at room temperature. Alternatively, mix the whole culinary lavender buds with the sugar and let it sit for 2 weeks. Mix occasionally to disperse the flavor. Remove the lavender buds with a sifter and store in an airtight container.

SIMPLE LAVENDER SYRUP
Makes 2 cups

Simple lavender syrup is an easy and delightful infusion that enhances just about any drink. Pour some in lemonades and teas. Add a shot to your next margarita or cosmopolitan. (Most recipes call for one ounce or one shot of lavender syrup per eight ounces of beverage. Adjust the amount you use according to taste.) It will transform your beverage from average to exceptional. This recipe is borrowed from Sharon Shipley's *The Lavender Cookbook*.

1 cup distilled or filtered water
1 cup sugar
2 tablespoons whole culinary
   lavender buds
1 strip lemon zest

❧ Boil the water in a small saucepan and add the sugar. Stir constantly until the sugar is dissolved. Add the culinary lavender buds and the lemon zest and allow the mixture to steep, uncovered, for about 30 minutes. Strain the mixture through a fine-screened colander or cheesecloth. Lavender syrup will keep in the refrigerator for up to 2 weeks.

Lavender syrup

Strawberry freezer jam
with lavender

LAVENDER-INFUSED JAM
Makes about 5 half pints (8 ounces each)

Lavender-infused jam or jelly has been a staple in our household. We have used berries, plums, and peaches to create a delicious lavender-infused spread for our favorite breakfast pastries.

1½ cups sugar
1 package (1.59 ounces) freezer jam fruit pectin
4 cups crushed strawberries, marionberries, raspberries,
  or whatever fruit is in season
2 teaspoons crushed culinary lavender
½ tablespoon finely grated lemon zest
5 8-ounce freezer jars

1. Stir the sugar and the pectin together in a bowl until well blended.

2. Add the fruit, the lavender, and the lemon zest. Stir 3 minutes.

3. Ladle the jam into clean jars to the fill line. Twist on the lids. Let stand until thickened, about 30 minutes. Refrigerate up to 3 weeks or freeze up to 1 year.

HERBAL VINEGAR WITH LAVENDER

Herbal vinegars are a fun and useful way to enjoy the bounty of your garden harvest throughout the year. Vinegars are not just for salads. They are also a healthy alternative for adding flavor to dishes as they contain no salt, preservatives, or significant calories. Drizzle them on fruit or use them to baste meats on the grill.

1. Harvest herbs at the peak of freshness by cutting them before they flower, preferably in the morning. Rinse the herbs thoroughly and allow them to dry completely.

2. Place the herbs in wide-mouth jars such as mason jars and pour in vinegar to cover all the vegetation completely. Some items may want to float to the top; if so, use a wooden skewer to keep them in place. Seal the jars tightly, placing waxed paper or plastic wrap between the lid and the jar to prevent rusting.

3. Allow the jars to sit for a period of time in a cool, dark place from 1 week to a few months to infuse the vinegar. The longer it sits, the more potent your vinegar will be, so don't let it sit more than about 6 months.

4. Strain the herbs from the vinegar using cheesecloth, muslin, or a paper coffee filter. Funnel the infused vinegar into containers. You can add fresh herbs to the new containers for decoration. Cap tightly and store in a cool, dark area. Herbal vinegars will last 6 to 8 months.

Apple cider vinegar
with fresh herbs

Some Ideas for Herbal Vinegar Combinations

You can use many different types of vinegars as a base. It is best to pair milder vinegars with less potent herbs and heartier vinegars with more robust herbs. A few lighter vinegars that go well with traditional herbs such as lavender and basil are champagne, cider, and rice vinegars. Herbs such as sage and rosemary complement wine vinegars, though white wine vinegar goes well with almost anything. Distilled vinegar is the most common and is used in pickling but is not suitable for herbal vinegar because the flavor is a bit harsh.

Here are some ideas for combining herbs and vinegars:

- lavender, lemon verbena, and thyme with champagne vinegar
- purple basil and garlic with white wine vinegar
- bay leaves, lemon balm, lavender, and shallots with apple cider vinegar
- rosemary, oregano, sage, parsley, garlic, and red pepper with red wine vinegar
- lavender, calendula, lemon thyme, and basil with rice vinegar

HERBAL COOKING OILS

Herbed oils can be used in a variety of ways. Pour herbed oil on a plate with a dash of pepper and dip crusty bread in it. Sauté garlic in it when making your favorite sauce or sprinkle it on a salad for a zesty taste. The proportion of oil to herb is important in relation to strength and taste of the finished product, so use the guidelines here to start and then experiment on your own with different combinations and strengths. Use lavender on its own or in combination with other herbs in varying proportions to taste.

½ cup cleaned and chopped fresh herb sprigs or leaves, or ¼ cup dried
1 cup of oil (olive, safflower, or sunflower)

1. Place the herbs in a nonmetal pan with the oil and gently sauté until the mixture is fragrant and warm—about 5 minutes. Do not let this mixture come to a boil.

2. Strain, place in decorative bottles, and store in the refrigerator. These oils should be made as needed and stored for no more than 3 weeks.

A sprig of rosemary flavoring an oil

Lavender Desserts

If you have visited a trendy restaurant lately, chances are you have found a lavender dessert on the menu. Lavender-infused desserts are becoming popular, and these recipes will allow you to try making them yourself. Simply delicious.

LAVENDER SHORTBREAD COOKIES WITH LEMON BUTTER CREAM FROSTING
Makes about 2 dozen cookies

This recipe is a slight variation on an old favorite. The lemon butter cream frosting adds moisture to the cookie, and the lavender sprinkles make for a nice presentation.

1½ cups (3 sticks) butter (not margarine), room temperature
⅔ cup sugar
2 teaspoons dried culinary lavender buds, chopped
2⅓ cups flour
½ cup cornstarch
¼ teaspoon salt

Frosting:
⅓ cup softened butter
½ teaspoon lemon zest
3 cups powdered sugar, sifted
2 tablespoons lemon juice

1. Preheat the oven to 325° F. Cover two baking sheets with parchment or brown paper.

2. In a large bowl with an electric mixer, cream together the butter, sugar, and lavender until light and fluffy, about 3 minutes. Add the flour, cornstarch, and salt; beat until combined.

3. Divide the dough in half. Flatten it into squares and wrap it in plastic. Chill in the refrigerator until firm, approximately 1 hour.

4. On a floured board, roll or pat out each square to a thickness of ⅜ inch. Cut the dough into 1½-inch rounds or into a shape of your choice with a cookie cutter.

4. Transfer the cookies to the prepared baking sheets, spacing the cookies about 1 inch apart. Prick each cookie several times with the tines of a fork. Bake 20 to 25 minutes until pale golden (do not brown). Cool slightly, then transfer to a rack. Allow the cookies to cool.

5. To make the frosting, cream together the softened butter and the lemon zest. Begin adding small amounts of the sugar and the lemon juice, mixing well before adding more.

6. Use a knife to spread the frosting on the cooled cookies. Before the frosting hardens, sprinkle lavender buds on top of each cookie.

Shortbread cookies flavored with lavender and frosted with lemon butter cream

LAVENDER CRÈME BRÛLÉE
Serves 4 or 5 (depending on the size of your custard cups)

This crème brûlée is infused with the flavor of lavender. The custard is baked in a water bath. The most common mistake people make in baking a custard is not putting enough water in the baking dish. The water should come up to where the level of the custard is inside the cups in order to protect your custard from the heat. Thanks to Purple Dog Farms, Finger Lakes, New York, for this recipe.

2 cups heavy cream
½ tablespoon dried lavender flowers
1 teaspoon vanilla
4 egg yolks
¼ cup granulated sugar
extra granulated sugar for the topping

1. Preheat the oven to 300° F. Butter (6-ounce) custard cups and set them in a glass baking dish with a layer of newspaper or kitchen cloth in the bottom to keep the cups from sliding (I use a silicone baking sheet).

2. In a saucepan over medium heat, heat the cream and the lavender flowers just to a simmer. Remove from the heat, add the vanilla, and allow the lavender flowers to infuse the cream for 5 minutes. Strain the cream mixture through a mesh strainer to remove the lavender flowers.

3. In a separate bowl, mix the egg yolks and the sugar together, then slowly pour a steady stream of the hot milk mixture into the egg yolks and sugar, stirring continuously.

4. Bring water for the water bath to a light simmer on top of the stove; carefully pour enough hot water into the baking dish to come half-way up the sides of the custard cups.

5. Bake 45 minutes or until the custard is set around the edges but still loose in the center. The cooking time will depend largely on the size of the custard cups you are using, but begin checking after 30 minutes and check back regularly. When the center of the custard is just set and jiggles a little when shaken, remove it from the oven.

6. Leave the cups in the water bath until cooled. Then remove the cups and refrigerate at least 2 hours. Use within 3 days.

7. When ready to serve, sprinkle approximately 2 teaspoons of sugar over each crème brûlée. I swirl the dish gently to evenly spread the sugar. For best results, use a small hand-held torch to melt the sugar. Hold the torch 4 to 5 inches from the sugar, maintaining a slow and even motion. Stop torching just before the desired degree of doneness is reached, as the sugar will continue to cook for a few seconds after the flame has been removed. If you don't have a torch, place the crème brûlée 6 inches below the broiler for 4 to 6 minutes or until the sugar bubbles and turns golden brown.

LAVENDER AND
LEMON VERBENA ICE CREAM
Makes 1 quart

At the farm we made 14 gallons of this ice cream for our lavender festival one year and it was gone before noon. It's simply delicious. If you can't find lemon verbena, you can substitute the zest of two lemons.

¾ cup granulated sugar
½ cup packed fresh lemon verbena leaves or the zest of
  2 lemons
¼ cup fresh lavender or ⅛ cup dried culinary lavender buds
2 cups whole milk
2 cups heavy cream
8 egg yolks
sprigs of fresh lavender and lemon verbena for garnish

1. In a medium saucepan, combine the sugar, lemon verbena leaves, lavender, milk, and cream. Bring to a boil and steep for 20 minutes covered. Strain the mixture through a fine-screened colander or cheesecloth to remove the leaves and buds. In another bowl, whisk the egg yolks.

2. Whisk 1 cup of the hot cream mixture into the egg yolks. Slowly whisk this new mixture into the remaining cream mixture in the saucepan. Stir constantly over low heat until the mixture is thick enough to coat the back of a wooden spoon.

3. Immediately remove from the heat and cool in an ice water bath or refrigerator until completely cool. Add the mixture to an electric ice cream maker. Process according to the manufacturers' directions.

LAVENDER CHOCOLATE TRUFFLES
Makes about 3 dozen

We have had the good fortune of providing culinary lavender to local chefs around the region who have allowed us to taste their scrumptious creations. Lavender chocolate truffles are a hands-down favorite and are usually gone within the hour. This recipe comes from my talented friend Eleanor Suman of Eleanor's Signature Catering.

> **6 ounces heavy cream**
> **1 tablespoon finely ground dried culinary lavender**
> **6 ounces semisweet chocolate, chopped fine**
> **powdered sugar**
> **4 ounces bittersweet chocolate, melted and cooled to 90° F**
> **cocoa powder, 1 rounded teaspoon for each truffle**

1. Over medium heat, mix the cream and the lavender together and bring to a boil. Remove from the heat and strain immediately into the chopped chocolate in a small mixing bowl. Let the mixture sit for 5 minutes without stirring. After 5 minutes, stir until the chocolate is completely melted and the ganache (chocolate mixture) is smooth. Cover the ganache with plastic wrap and chill until firm, about 2 hours.

2. Line a baking sheet with parchment or waxed paper. Scoop balls from the ganache with a melon baller dipped in powdered sugar. Quickly firm the balls between your palms and coat in the melted bittersweet chocolate. Roll in the cocoa powder to finish.

3. Place the truffles on the prepared baking sheet. Chill until firm, at least 2 hours. Truffles can be made 2 weeks ahead. Store them in an airtight container in the refrigerator. Dust them once more with cocoa powder before serving if needed.

Lavender-Flavored Beverages

At our local lavender festivals, the lavender lemonade stand always has a long line. Lavender is delicious in beverages, and when brewed into a tea has medicinal benefits as well. I encourage you to experiment with what lavender can do for your body and spirit.

LAVENDER LEMONADE
Serves 6

You can prepare plain lemonade and then add lavender syrup (see the recipe earlier in this chapter) or make it from scratch as this recipe specifies. Either way, get ready to make copies of this recipe for whoever tries it.

**4 cups filtered water
1 cup sugar or honey
2 tablespoons dried lavender buds or
     4 tablespoons fresh lavender
1 cup lemon juice, freshly squeezed
Lavender sprigs for garnish**

1. Combine the water, sugar or honey, and lavender in a saucepan and heat for approximately 10 minutes or until the mixture begins to boil. Remove from the heat and allow to steep until cool, about 20 minutes.

2. Pour the mixture through a fine-screened colander or cheesecloth into a pitcher. Add the lemon juice and stir. Serve in glasses filled with ice and garnished with a lavender sprig or lemon wheel.

A cold glass of lavender lemonade on a hot summer day

WARM HOLIDAY SPICE PUNCH
Serves 6 to 8

This delicious beverage has proved a favorite at holiday parties. The punch can be made in a slow cooker and left on simmer throughout your event or gathering.

> 3 cups cranberry juice
> 1 cup apple juice
> 1 cup orange juice
> 1 cup water
> ¼ cup sugar or 2 tablespoons honey
> 2 tablespoons fresh lemon juice
> 3 small cinnamon sticks
> 2 cloves
> dash of cinnamon
> 2 tablespoons dried culinary lavender buds

✤ In a saucepan or slow cooker, combine all the ingredients and allow them to simmer over medium heat. The spices can remain in the punch or can be strained out.

Lavender and
chamomile tea

HERBAL TEAS WITH LAVENDER

Herbal teas are an all-natural way to get the healing benefits of herbs. Hot or iced, plain or sweetened, herbal teas can calm you down at the end of a long day or give you an organic boost when you need it. Lavender tea is wonderful all by itself and works as well as chamomile to quiet the nerves. Adding a bit of lemon and honey makes it that much better.

You can purchase bulk teas from your local health food store or snip fresh herbs straight from your garden. Depending on the herb, teas can be made from the leaves of the plant or, as with lavender, from the flowers and buds. How much to use is a matter of personal preference. Before using a particular herb, it is important do your research. Healing benefits and properties have been passed down for centuries, but some herbs may have side effects.

Teas can be prepared by making tea bags or by using a spoon infuser. Simply add the herbs you want to use, fresh or dried, and steep for a few minutes in hot water.

Herbs for Common Ailments

The following list of common ailments gives the herbs that have been known to help with symptoms. There is a great deal of information available on the subject of herbs and health. I encourage you to find what may work well for you, but this is not a substitute for professional medical advice.

Allergies: feverfew, ginkgo, lemon balm, thyme
Colds: echinacea, ginger, goldenseal, lavender
Depression: ginseng, lavender, oat straw, St. John's wort
Dizziness: ginger, ginkgo, lavender, peppermint
Fever: burdock, echinacea, lavender, yarrow
Headaches: feverfew, ginkgo, lavender, milk thistle, rosemary
High blood pressure: ginger, ginseng, hawthorn, yarrow
Immunity: echinacea, ginkgo, oat straw, rose hips
Laryngitis: fennel, lavender, peppermint
Nervous tension: lavender, motherwort, passion flower, rose hips, scullcap
Skin health: calendula, echinacea, lavender, oat straw, red clover, thyme

Scented Creations:

Wands, Wreaths,
Swags, Sachets,
and Beyond

Fresh herbs can dry in
place in a colorful herb box

The uses for lavender in crafting and aromatherapy are endless. Lavender oil is also a fragrant additive to home care and cosmetic creations. I highlight a few classic projects here that will bring the luscious scent and color of lavender into your home.

Best Lavenders for Crafts

Want to make a dried bouquet or try your hand at a lavender wreath? Choose from these lavenders for best color and staying power.

Lavandula angustifolia 'Betty's Blue'
L. angustifolia 'Purple Bouquet'
L. angustifolia 'Royal Velvet'
L. angustifolia 'Seal's Seven Oaks'
L. ×intermedia 'Gros Bleu'

Preparing to make
lavender wands

LAVENDER WANDS

Lavender wands, also called lavender bottles, were fashioned in Victorian times for scenting drawers and cabinets. Thankfully, they are making a comeback. Lavender wands are worth the effort it takes to make them because they allow you to encase the scent of lavender in ribbon and enjoy the fragrance for years to come. Taking the time to create wands allows you to get lost in the moment while enjoying the aroma as you weave the ribbon around the stalks of lavender. They also make wonderful homemade gifts.

> **thin ribbon, approximately ½ inch thick, in any color you want, about 1 yard per wand**
> **an odd number of fresh lavender stems from _Lavandula ×intermedia_ varieties such as 'Grosso' or 'Provence'; start with 15 to 17 stems to make a good-sized wand; you may want to increase the number once you master the technique**
> **scissors to cut the ribbon**

1. Gather the lavender stems together, making the heads even at the top with the stems facing downward.

2. Tie a knot with your ribbon around the base of the lavender heads.

3. Flip the lavender heads upside down and one by one bend the lavender stems down as if you were peeling a banana. Use your fingernail

to gently bend the stems over the lavender heads, being careful not to break them. Try to bend them evenly around the lavender flowers. This will help later as you begin to weave the ribbon.

4. The knot you tied at the bottom of the lavender heads should now be at the top. Here's the tricky part. Begin weaving your ribbon between the lavender stems using an over-under pattern. As you are doing this, try to keep the stems evenly spaced around the flower heads to create uniformity. By the time you come around thelavender heads the first time, you should have gone either over or under each stem one time.

5. After the first pass, continue to weave the ribbon over and under each stem. If you are doing this correctly, a pattern should emerge, encasing the lavender in your ribbon. If you come to a place where you missed a stem, undo the ribbon and try to find where you missed one.

6. Eventually you will reach the bottom of the flower heads, and they should be completely wrapped in ribbon. Wrap the ribbon around the bottom and tie a tight knot. Cut off the remaining ribbon. You can also use the additional ribbon to make another knot at the bottom of the stems so they don't stick out.

Bending the stems over the lavender heads

Weaving the ribbon over and under.

Continuing to weave the ribbon

A lavender hurricane,
another use for your
lavender wreath

LAVENDER WREATHS

I have chosen to illustrate the classic lavender wreath here; however, you can mix in any combination of flowers and herbs when making a wreath. Wreath frames come in all shapes and sizes, from circles to squares and even hearts. I like to use dried lavender when I make a wreath because fresh lavender shrinks when it dries, making it more likely that the lavender will fall out of the places you have tucked it. The wreath frame pictured here is an 8-inch frame, meaning it measures 8 inches across. When your wreath is complete, it should measure approximately 12 inches across.

wreath frame in the size you want, purchased at just about any craft store
thin floral wire
scissors or pruning shears for trimming the lavender stems and wire
approximately six to eight bunches of dried lavender, depending on how thick you want to make your wreath

1. Gather approximately 15 to 20 stems of lavender and cut the stems to leave a 6- to 8-inch bunch of lavender.

2. Tie your wire to the wreath frame and unwrap the wire about 8 inches in preparation for your first bunch.

3. Place your trimmed bunch on the wreath frame, tilting the lavender slightly to the side, and use the wire to wrap the lavender bunch, securing it tightly to the wreath frame. Wrap it around once more.

4. Cut another bunch the same size as the first one and place it at an angle on top of the first bunch. Wrap the wire around the second bunch, securing it tightly to the wreath frame.

5. Continue to use this technique while adding bunches and eventually coming all the way around the wreath frame.

6. Once you reach the end, try to secure the last bunch in such a way that it will not leave a gap. You may have to move your lavender flowers around a bit to make it look uniform.

7. When your wreath is complete, you can either hang it on a nail directly or fashion a loop with some additional wire.

Securing the first bunch to the wreath frame

After the second bunch has been secured

The completed lavender wreath

LAVENDER-AND-WHEAT SHEAF

Bring the feel of Provence into your home with a lavender-and-wheat sheaf. They are easy to make and are a great focal point on a dining room table.

> **approximately two good-sized bunches of dried lavender; varieties of *Lavandula angustifolia* or *L. ×intermedia* will work just fine**
> **good-sized bunch of traditional wheat or black-bearded wheat**
> **thin raffia**

1. Loosen your lavender bunch and begin interspersing it with the wheat, making an even bouquet.
2. Twist the lavender and wheat together, splaying out the bottom into an even circle.
3. Work with your bouquet until it can stand up on a table. At this point you can either wrap a rubber band around the middle to keep it secure or tie raffia around the middle a few times and tie it into a knot.

Lavender-and-wheat sheaf

Lavender herb box
containing various
mixed herbs

HERB BOX

You can use just about any container—wooden, metal, plastic,
ceramic—to make an herb box. Boxes come in all shapes and sizes.
This version uses fresh herbs but you can use dried herbs as well.

> **container of your choice**
> **wired wood floral picks, available at most craft stores**
> **florist styrofoam**
> **sharp knife**
> **collection of herbs of your choosing**

1. Gather herbs together in clumps, keeping the stems about 4 to 6
   inches long, depending on the type of herb.
2. Wrap the wire from a pick around one clump of herbs. Use a different pick for each clump.
3. Lay florist styrofoam at the bottom of your container and trim with
   your knife for easy insertion.
4. Taking the container in sections, begin to insert your wood picks
   into the styrofoam while keeping your herb clumps upright.
5. Once your herb box is full, you can allow the herbs to dry in the
   container or use fresh in the kitchen for a time.

HERB SWAG

Herb swag

I love this swag because it can hang in the kitchen, allowing you to snip herbs for use in recipes. Choose for your swag the herbs you use most in cooking. Rosemary and lavender look great together, as do sage and thyme. Mix and match for creative color schemes.

10 strips of raffia, each approximately 3 feet long, plus extra strips to tie at the top later
floral wire
herbs of your choosing (fresh or dried)

1. Lay out raffia strips together evenly and gather them in the middle, making a 1-inch loop. Braid the strips to the bottom, leaving a bit loose at the end.

2. Start at the bottom of your braid by bundling the first set of herbs together and wrapping tightly with floral wire. This will be the largest number of herbs you want to use. As you work your way up, make your herb bundles smaller and smaller. Keep in mind that fresh herbs will shrink when dried, so keep your wire tight or use dried herbs to alleviate this issue.

3. Continue to add herbs as you work your way up the swag, fanning your herbs out as you go along.

4. Once you reach the top of the swag, tie your last bunch, then use leftover raffia to wrap around the top several times. Tie at the back or secure with a glue gun.

Fire starters ready for use
in the fireplace or grill

LAVENDER FIRE STARTERS

One way to bring the scent of lavender into your home during the winter months is to make lavender fire starters. Lavender stems, especially those of lavandins, still smell like lavender, and can be used in your fireplace as scented kindling. The intoxicating aroma will be released into your home. During the summer you can soak them in water and put them on the fire in your grill. After they burn, the smoky scent will flavor your food.

> **thick bundle of lavender stems, approximately 150**
> **pruning shears**
> **raffia or twine**
> **scissors**

1. Gather a bundle of lavender stems and use pruning shears to cut the stems to the length of your choice so they are even on both ends.

2. Tie raffia or twine on both ends to hold the bundle together. Cut with scissors.

3. Make as many as you want and store above your fireplace. Throw the entire bundle into the fire as needed.

LAVENDER OIL CONCOCTIONS

Lavender oil

Pure lavender essential oil is extracted from flowers using a process called steam distillation. This process separates the oil from the steam, leaving the pure essence of the flower. *Lavandula angustifolia* and *L. ×intermedia* varieties are used to make oil. Since *L. angustifolia* cultivars are low in camphor and tend to carry a more floral note, oil extracted from this species tends to cost more. With its sharper, woodier fragrance, oil from *L. ×intermedia* varieties is used more frequently in household cleaning products and bath and body cosmetics. *Lavandula angustifolia* oils on the market are usually labeled with the species name or "English lavender"; oils from *L. ×intermedia* are labeled with that name or "lavandin oil." Which oil you choose is a matter of personal preference. Remember not to add lavender oil distilled from *L. ×intermedia* varieties to food as it contains camphor and has a bitter taste. *Lavandula angustifolia* oil can be used in very small amounts in food, but remember that a little goes a long way.

The Many Uses of Lavender Oil

Here are some uses for lavender oil around the home:

◈ Add a few drops to your mop water for fragrance and antiseptic benefits.

◈ Put some in your bath water.

◈ Add a few drops to your massage oil.

◈ Add to a diffuser and fill your room with the scent of lavender.

◈ Keep it in your medicine cabinet for burns, cuts, insect bites, and to help reduce scaring.

◈ Use it as a solvent to remove glue left over from price stickers or labels.

◈ Add a few drops of oil to a compress to ease a headache.

◈ Dab a few drops behind your ears to use as a natural cologne.

◈ Add a few drops to steaming water and lean over it, covering your head with a towel, to give yourself a facial or help clear congestion.

◈ Add it to any natural face mask to detoxify and shrink pores.

◈ Mix it with water and apply to sunburned skin to help cool the burn.

◈ Put a few drops on your dog or cat bed as a natural flea repellant and as a natural sleep aid.

◈ Mix a few drops with olive oil for a hair tonic. It will leave your hair silky and disinfect your scalp (it will kill lice, lice eggs, and nits).

◈ Put a few drops on the affected area to help control athlete's foot, eczema, dermatitis, and acne with its antibacterial and antiseptic properties.

◈ Put a few drops on a clean cloth tossed into your dryer and infuse the scent of lavender into your laundry.

◈ Dab a few drops on pressure points to relieve anxiety, depression, emotional stress, and exhaustion.

Natural ingredients to mix
into an all-purpose cleaner

ALL-PURPOSE CLEANER
Makes 14 ounces

The word *lavender* comes from the Latin *lavar*, meaning to wash. Long
before the antimicrobial properties of lavender were discovered, it was
used in solutions for bathing and housecleaning. Now you can add it
to an all-purpose cleaner made from common household ingredients to
impart a pleasing aroma and all the disinfectant benefits. You can also
add lemon essential oil or juice to cleaners to make them capable of
deodorizing and removing stains while giving them a clean lemony scent.

Many people are beginning to switch to natural cleaners for good
reason. The average household uses about 40 pounds of toxic household chemicals a year—chemicals that not only do damage to our environment but also contain volatile organic compounds (VOCs) that can
make indoor air unhealthy. Making your own cleaners will help the environment and your health, and they are inexpensive alternatives to store-

bought cleaners. Borax can be purchased at most grocery stores; it is an all-purpose cleaner with many benefits but it can be toxic if ingested, so store it in a locked cabinet and keep it away from children and pets. Castile soap can be found in most grocery stores or online.

2 tablespoons distilled white vinegar
1 teaspoon borax
distilled or purified water
¼ cup liquid castile soap
10 drops lavender essential oil
5 drops lemon essential oil or 1 teaspoon lemon juice

1. Mix the white vinegar and the borax together in a 16-ounce bottle. Fill the bottle three-quarters full with hot purified or distilled water. Shake well until the borax is dissolved.

2. Add the liquid castile soap and the essential oils (or the lavender oil and the lemon juice) to the solution and shake well. Use as you would any other all-purpose cleaner.

Oatmeal and lavender
for a restorative
cleanser or mask

OATMEAL AND LAVENDER RESTORATIVE
Makes one application

Tired of spending ridiculous amounts of money for face creams, masks, and cleansers? Here is a natural, cost-effective daily cleaner, face mask, and body scrub all in one from *Organic Body Care Recipes* by Stephanie Tourles. It's easy to make and works wonders on your skin. The lavender adds scent and antiseptic benefits. To use as a body scrub, triple the recipe. Do not store for later use.

1 tablespoon oat flour or oatmeal ground fine (a food processor works well)
purified water
2 drops lavender essential oil or 1 tablespoon lavender buds

1. Combine the oat flour or oatmeal in a small bowl with enough water to create a smooth paste. Add the lavender oil to the mixture and stir well. Alternatively, add the oatmeal and lavender buds along with a little water to a food processor and mix well.

2. Using your fingers, spread the mixture on your face and massage well. Rinse with water to use it as a face cleanser, or leave it on for 20 minutes and rinse to use as a face mask.

LAVENDER SUGAR SCRUB
Makes 12 ounces

Finely granulated sugar can be used as a gentle exfoliant and is sometimes preferred over sea salt because it is less abrasive. Sugar has natural glycolic acids, found in many cosmetic products. Sugar scrubs can be used on the body, but avoid sensitive, irritated, or sunburned skin. Adding vitamin E oil will prolong the life of your sugar scrub. Make sure you store your scrub out of direct sunlight.

⅔ cup jojoba oil, unrefined or cold pressed (check the label)
10 drops lavender essential oil
½ teaspoon vitamin E oil (optional)
½ teaspoon vanilla extract (optional)
1 cup finely granulated white sugar or brown coarse sugar
1 12-ounce mason jar with lid or glass jar with tight-fitting cover

1. Add the wet ingredients to a mixing bowl and stir well.

2. Pour the sugar in all at once. Stir until the sugar is moistened and the mixture is smooth.

3. Pour into the jar and seal.

A sugar scrub made with lavender oil

LAVENDER SPRAY

Lavender spray: easy to make, versatile to use

Lavender-infused water is a recipe that has been passed down for centuries. It is easy to make and the uses are endless. Spray it on linens, laundry, or furniture. A light spritz on children's pillows will help them sleep. Keep a bottle in the glove box to spritz yourself and calm your nerves before you go into a big meeting. Use it in your iron as a substitute for plain distilled water.

To infuse the water, you can use lavender oil or else boil fresh or dried lavender with water and strain; either way works well.

A note about staining: If you put too much lavender essential oil in the mix, it may stain, so use only a few drops. If you make the spray with fresh or dried lavender, the water will be tinted slightly purple; test it on an area first before you spray to make sure it does not stain.

LAVENDER WATER WITH ESSENTIAL OIL
Makes 8 ounces or 1 cup

1 cup distilled water
2 teaspoons plain vodka or witch hazel as a preservative
5 drops lavender essential oil

❧ Mix the ingredients together and shake well. Pour into a glass or plastic 8-ounce spray bottle. This formula will last up to 8 weeks. Keep in the refrigerator for prolonged use.

LAVENDER WATER MADE WITH FRESH OR DRIED LAVENDER
Makes 8 ounces or 1 cup

1½ cups fresh lavender or ¾ cup dried lavender buds
1½ cups distilled water or mineral water
¼ cup plain vodka or witch hazel as a preservative

❧ Simmer the lavender in the water in a large heavy saucepan for 10 minutes, stirring occasionally. Remove the pan from the heat and allow the mixture to steep until cool. Using cheesecloth, strain the mixture into a separate container. Add the vodka or witch hazel and shake well.

A sewn lavender sachet

LAVENDER DRYER SACHETS

Traditional dryer sheets can be expensive and add unwanted chemicals to your laundry. Lavender dryer bags can be used for up to ten full dryer cycles and will leave your clothes with the fresh scent of lavender. You can make your own either by sewing the bags or by using sealable tea bags. Sealable tea bags can be purchased in various sizes and quantities. They can be used not only for dryer bags but also for hot tea, potpourri, and bath salts.

For sewn bags:
all-cotton fabric (unbleached muslin is a good choice)
a template in your choice of shape; squares or
**   hearts work fine**
scissors
sewing machine or needle and thread
pins to hold the fabric together
loose dried lavender buds (using a stronger-smelling
**   variety such as *Lavandula* ×*intermedia* 'Grosso' will make**
**   the scent last longer)**

1. Fold the fabric in two and cut around the template with scissors (you will have two identical pieces).

2. Pin the pieces together and sew close to the edges, leaving a 2-inch opening on one side. Make sure your stitches are tight to keep the lavender from spilling out.

3. Turn the pouch right side out and fill with loose lavender buds. Sew the opening shut.

> **With sealable tea bags:**
> **sealable tea bags purchased in 4- by 5-inch or**
>   **5- by 5-inch sizes**
> **muslin drawstring bags large enough to hold a tea bag**
> **loose dried lavender buds (using a stronger-smelling**
>   **variety such as *Lavandula* ×*intermedia* 'Grosso' will make**
>   **the scent last longer)**
> **an iron for heat-sealing the tea bags**

1. Fill tea bags with loose lavender buds. Make sure not to stuff the bags too tightly since the buds will expand when wet. Iron the open end until sealed.

2. Place each tea bag in a muslin bag and cinch tightly. You may want to add a few stitches to the muslin bag in case the tea bag breaks.

3. Once the scent dissipates, discard the used tea bag and replace with another in the muslin bag.

Resources

Lavender Associations and Festivals

For a current list of lavender associations and festivals being held at various locations around the globe, go to www.lavenderatstonegate.com. What follows is a list of major festivals and associations.

Canada

Ontario Lavender Association: Supporting the development of the lavender industry in Ontario. www.ontariolavenderassociation.com.

France

Lavander of Provence: Guide to the "Route de la lavande," passing through small villages "where the scent of lavender is everywhere in the wind," and to lavender festivals and events in Provence. www.provenceweb.fr/e/mag/terroir/lavande.htm.

New Zealand

New Zealand Lavender Growers Association: Promoting quality oil and products for the New Zealand lavender industry. www.lavender.org.nz.

At Barn Owl Nursery

United Kingdom

Downderry Nursery, Kent: Summer tours of the nursery and fields in July and August. www.downderry-nursery.co.uk/.

The Hop Shop at Castle Farm, Kent: Lavender festival on the first two weekends of July. Prebooked tours in June and July. www.hopshop.co.uk/.

Isle of Wight Lavender, Isle of Wight: Lavender fields and distillery open to visitors. National Collection holder for *Lavandula* with more than 230 varieties. www.lavender.co.uk/.

Jersey Lavender, Jersey, Channel Islands: Open to visitors. Talks during harvest season. www.jerseylavender.co.uk/.

Norfolk Lavender, Norfolk: Lavender fields, distillery, museum, and herb garden open to visitors. National Collection holder with more than 100 varieties. www.norfolk-lavender.co.uk/.

Shropshire Lavender, Shropshire: Festival in July. Lavender fields and other attractions open to visitors. www.shropshirelavender.co.uk/.

Snowshill Lavender, Worcestershire: Lavender fields and distillery open to visitors. www.snowshill-lavender.co.uk/.

United Kingdom *(continued)*

Yorkshire Lavender, Yorkshire: Garden and other attractions open to visitors. www.yorkshirelavender.com.

United States

Arizona Lavender Festival, Red Rock Ranch, Concho, Arizona: See website for dates and times. www.redrockfarms.com.

Blanco Lavender Festival, Blanco, Texas: Free farm tours; lavender market and speakers' pavilion located on the grounds of the Blanco County Courthouse. www.blancolavenderfest.com.

Central Coast Lavender Festival, Paso Robles, California: Takes place in the downtown city park on the second weekend in July. www.central-coastlavenderfestival.com. Organized by the **Central Coast Lavender Growers Association**, www.cclga.org.

Colorado Lavender Festival, Palisades, Colorado: Held on the third weekend in July. Self-guided farm tours on Friday, festival in Palisade Memorial Park on Saturday. www.coloradolavender.org/lavenderfestival.html. Organized by the **Lavender Association of Western Colorado**, www.coloradolavender.org.

Ojai Valley Lavender Festival, Ojai, California: Held on the fourth Saturday in June at Libbey Park. www.ojaivalleylavenderfestival.org.

Oregon Lavender Festival: A self-guided tour covering farms in Oregon. Always the second weekend in July.

www.oregonlavenderdestinations.org. Organized by the **Oregon Lavender Association**, www.oregonlavender.org.

Pennsylvania Lavender Festival, Fairfield, Pennsylvania: Workshops, lectures, and tours. Held every June at Willow Pond Farm. www.palavenderfestival.com.

Sequim Lavender Farm Faire, Sequim, Washington: Held at Carrie Blake Park the third weekend in July. Farm tours leave from Carrie Blake Park to visit the major lavender farms in Sequim, which bills itself as the Lavender Capital of North America. www.sequimlavenderfarms.org. Organized by the **Sequim Lavender Farmers Association**, www.sequimlavenderfarmersassociation.org.

Sequim Lavender Festival, Sequim, Washington: Always the third weekend in July. Self-guided farm tours and street fair put on by the Sequim Lavender Growers Association. www.lavenderfestival.com.

Texas Lavender Association: Promotes the research, education, growth, market development, and distribution of lavender and lavender products. www.texaslavenderassociation.org.

United States Lavender Growers Association: A national organization to support and promote the U.S. lavender industry through research, education, networking, and marketing. www.uslavender.com

Mail-Order Plant Companies

United Kingdom

Norfolk Lavender Farm: Retail mail-order
  nursery for lavender plants and products
  Caley Mill
  Heacham
  King's Lynn
  Norfolk
  PE31 7JE
  0845 345 1383
  orders@norfolk-lavender.co.uk
  www.norfolk-lavender.co.uk/

Isle of Wight Lavender: Retail mail-order
  nursery for lavender plants and products
  Staplehurst Grange
  Staplers Road
  Isle of Wight
  PO30 2LU
  0198 382 5272
  info@lavender.co.uk
  www.lavender.co.uk

United States

Goodwin Creek Gardens: Retail mail-order
  nursery for lavender and other herbs
  P.O. Box 83
  Williams, Oregon 97544
  800-846-7359
  info@goodwincreekgardens.com
  www.goodwincreekgardens.com

Joy Creek Nursery: Retail mail-order nursery
  for lavender and companion plants
  20300 NW Watson Road
  Scappoose, Oregon 97056
  503-543-7474
  catalogue@joycreek.com
  www.joycreek.com

Lavender at Stonegate: Retail mail-order
  nursery for the majority of lavender plants
  and products in this book
  22615 SW Ulsky Road
  West Linn, Oregon 97068
  888-638-5218
  info@lavenderatstonegate.com
  www.lavenderatstonegate.com

Further Reading

The Herb Companion, available on newsstands and online (www.herbcompanion.com), is a magazine that is always packed full of wonderful and useful information about herbs and all they have to offer. You might also enjoy these publications:

Dirr, Michael, and Charles W. Heuser Jr. 2006. *The Reference Manual of Woody Plant Propagation: From Seed to Tissue Culture*. 2nd ed. Portland, Oregon: Timber Press.

Evelegh, Tessa. 1996. *Lavender: Practical Inspirations for Natural Gifts, Country Crafts, and Decorative Displays*. New York, New York: Lorenz Books.

Gehrt, Kathy. 2010. *Discover Cooking with Lavender*. Seattle, Washington: Florentia Press.

Kehoe, Louise. 2010. Knot gardens. The Old Farmer's Almanac online, http://www.almanac.com/content/knot-gardens.

McNaughton, Virginia. 2010. *Lavender: The Grower's Guide*. Portland, Oregon: Timber Press. First edition, Bloomings Books Pty Ltd, Australia, 2000.

Shipley, Sharon. 2004. *The Lavender Cookbook*. Philadelphia, Pennsylvania: Running Press.

Tourles, Stephanie. 2007. *Organic Body Care Recipes: 175 Homemade Herbal Formulas for Glowing Skin and a Vibrant Self*. North Adams, Massachusetts: Storey Books.

Tucker, Arthur, and Thomas DeBaggio. 2009. *The Encyclopedia of Herbs: A Comprehensive Reference to Herbs of Flavor and Fragrance*. Portland, Oregon: Timber Press.

Upson, Tim, and Susyn Andrews. 2004. *The Genus Lavandula*. Portland, Oregon: Timber Press.

Vasich, Jennifer. 2009. *The Lavender Gourmet*. Mount Clemens, Michigan: Moose Run Productions.

Zak, Victoria. 1999. *20,000 Secrets of Tea: The Most Effective Ways to Benefit from Nature's Healing Herbs*. New York, New York: Dell.

Metric Conversions

INCHES	CM		FEET	M		TEMPERATURES
$\frac{1}{10}$	0.3		1	0.3		$°C = (\frac{5}{9} \times °F) - 32$
$\frac{1}{6}$	0.4		2	0.6		$°F = (\frac{9}{5} \times °C) + 32$
$\frac{1}{4}$	0.6		3	0.9		
$\frac{1}{3}$	0.8		4	1.2		
$\frac{1}{2}$	1.3		5	1.5		
$\frac{3}{4}$	1.9		6	1.8		
1	2.5		7	2.1		
2	5.1		8	2.4		
3	7.6		9	2.7		
4	10		10	3		
5	13		20	6		
6	15		30	9		
7	18		40	12		
8	20		50	15		
9	23		60	18		
10	25		70	21		
20	51		80	24		
30	76		90	27		
40	100		100	30		
50	130					
60	150					
70	180					
80	200					
90	230					
100	250					

Index

At Purple Haze
Lavender Farm,
Sequim, Washington

About the Author

"Every time I walk past a lavender plant, I take the time to rub the flowers, close my eyes, and inhale the calming aroma."

SARAH BERRINGER BADER has always been drawn to lavender. In 2000 she purchased a five-acre farm south of Portland, Oregon, and after visiting the Sequim Lavender Festival in Washington and seeing rows and rows of this wondrous herb, decided to create a test plot of 365 plants despite knowing nothing about planting lavender. She learned through trial and error, helped by a little-known society of lavender pioneers who had dedicated their careers to cultivating, growing, and preserving the true species of lavender. Soon she purchased many varieties of lavender from a seasoned grower in Oregon who had propagated starts from his own extensive collection acquired over a twenty-year span.

In 2005 she planted almost 5000 lavender plants with more than ninety cultivars and began propagating her own starts from cuttings. She opened her farm to the public and began holding the classes that inspired this book. Sarah and her farm, Lavender at Stonegate, have been featured in regional publications, on television and radio, and in *Grower Talks* and *Country Gardens* magazines.